This publication is intended solely for educational, analytical, informational, and professional development purposes. It does not constitute legal advice, medical advice, clinical treatment guidance, regulatory determination, or expert witness opinion. Readers should consult appropriately qualified legal, medical, regulatory, or professional advisors regarding specific matters.

The Lexcura Clinical Intelligence Model™ is a proprietary analytical framework developed for structured medical-legal evaluation, chronology reconstruction, operational analysis, causation assessment, escalation review, and litigation-oriented clinical intelligence.

Published by: Lexcura Summit Medical-Legal Analysts Gainesville, Florida, USA

Author: Michelle Carroll

Library of Congress Control Number: Pending

Copyright Registration: Pending

Paperback ISBN: 979-8-9962897-1-4

First Edition 2026

Trademark + Proprietary Methodology Notice

The Lexcura Clinical Intelligence Model™ is a proprietary analytical framework developed by Michelle Carroll and Lexcura Summit for structured medical-legal evaluation and healthcare litigation analysis.

The framework terminology, analytical structures, scoring concepts, methodologies, diagrams, and evaluation systems presented throughout this publication are proprietary intellectual property and may not be reproduced, taught, adapted into commercial training systems, incorporated into certification programs, or used within derivative analytical frameworks without prior written authorization.

Protected proprietary terminology includes, but is not limited to:

Lexcura Clinical Intelligence Model™
Record Integrity™
Baseline Profiling™
Timeline Reconstruction™
Regulatory & Compliance Overlay™
Causation Mapping™
Litigation-Ready Output™
Lexcura Case Exposure Index™ (LCEI™)
Lexcura Intake Integrity Score™ (LIIS™)

This publication is intended for authorized educational and professional use only.

The purchase or use of this book does not grant licensing rights, certification rights, implementation rights, or authorization to reproduce or commercially utilize the Lexcura Clinical Intelligence Model™ or associated proprietary methodologies.

All trademarks, methodology titles, framework terminology, and associated intellectual property remain the property of Michelle Carroll and Lexcura Summit unless otherwise indicated.

Licensing, certification, enterprise training, and authorized implementation inquiries may be directed to:

Lexcura Summit
Founder & Chief Clinical Strategist

Professional / Educational / Legal Disclaimer

This publication is intended solely for educational, analytical, and informational purposes within the field of medical-legal evaluation and healthcare litigation analysis.

The content presented in this book reflects the professional opinions, analytical methodologies, and clinical reasoning frameworks of the author based upon healthcare experience, medical-legal evaluation principles, and structured clinical intelligence methodology.

This publication is not intended to provide legal advice, medical advice, clinical treatment recommendations, regulatory determinations, or independent expert witness opinion for any specific matter, patient, claim, or litigation proceeding.

Readers should not rely upon this publication as a substitute for independent legal counsel, licensed medical evaluation, expert consultation, regulatory review, or case specific professional analysis.

Medical litigation analysis is highly fact-specific and depends upon the unique clinical circumstances, documentation, physiology, operational conditions, jurisdictional standards, evidentiary considerations, and expert interpretation present within each individual case.

The analytical concepts and methodologies presented in this publication are intended to support structured clinical intelligence evaluation and should not be interpreted as guaranteeing litigation outcome, legal strategy success, causation determination, regulatory finding, or standard-of-care conclusion in any specific matter.

The author and publisher make no representations or warranties regarding the completeness, applicability, or outcome of any analysis performed using the concepts discussed in this publication.

References to clinical scenarios, litigation analysis, operational failures, causation evaluation, regulatory considerations, or healthcare system processes are presented for educational and analytical illustration only.

Nothing contained within this publication establishes an attorney-client relationship, physician-patient relationship, consulting engagement, or formal expert retention relationship.

Readers remain responsible for obtaining appropriate professional guidance, independent expert review, and jurisdiction-specific legal or clinical consultation when evaluating actual medical-legal matters.

Confidentiality, Licensing & Training Notice

The Lexcura Clinical Intelligence Model™ is a proprietary analytical framework developed for structured medical-legal evaluation, litigation analysis, professional education, and authorized clinical intelligence training.

This publication is intended for individual educational and professional use unless otherwise authorized in writing by Michelle Carroll or Lexcura Summit.

The methodologies, framework terminology, analytical structures, scoring systems, and training concepts presented throughout this publication are proprietary intellectual property and may not be reproduced, adapted into independent certification programs, incorporated into commercial training systems, or implemented within derivative educational or consulting frameworks without prior written authorization.

Reviewing or purchasing this publication does not constitute certification, licensing, instructor authorization, implementation approval, or professional designation relating to the Lexcura Clinical Intelligence Model™.

Formal certification, licensing, enterprise training, and authorized implementation are available only through approved programs provided directly by Lexcura Summit.

Organizations, consultants, educators, and commercial entities seeking to incorporate the Lexcura Clinical Intelligence Model™ into internal operations, training systems, consulting services, or litigation support workflows must obtain appropriate licensing authorization prior to implementation or instructional use.

Certain certification programs, enterprise systems, and licensed training materials may contain additional proprietary methodologies, operational structures, scoring systems, and implementation frameworks not fully presented within this publication.
For licensing, certification, enterprise training, or implementation inquiries, contact:

Lexcura Summit

Founder & Chief Clinical Strategist

Author Note

Medical litigation often begins with a deceptively simple question:

What happened?

In complex healthcare cases, the answer is rarely straightforward.

Modern medical records may contain thousands of pages spread across multiple admissions, provider teams, electronic systems, reassessment notes, consultant evaluations, operative reports, and evolving clinical events occurring over days, weeks, or even months. Important findings may exist within the records while the overall clinical picture remains unclear.

Over time, I began noticing the same recurring problem in medical-legal review:

Large amounts of information were being analyzed without a consistent structure capable of connecting chronology, physiology, operational conditions, causation, and litigation strategy into one coherent understanding of the case.

That observation became one of the driving reasons the Lexcura Clinical Intelligence Model™ was developed.

The model was not created to amplify criticism or apply hindsight interpretation to difficult medical outcomes. It was developed to bring greater structure, discipline, and analytical clarity to the evaluation of complex healthcare litigation.

At its core, the framework asks a series of fundamental questions:

How did the deterioration evolve? When did meaningful intervention opportunity realistically exist? Which findings materially influenced the patient's trajectory? Which operational conditions affected the progression of care? And do the conclusions remain proportionate once the records undergo deeper physiologic and evidentiary analysis?

These questions require more than isolated record review. They require integrated clinical intelligence.

This book was written to introduce a structured methodology for evaluating medical litigation through chronology reconstruction, baseline profiling, operational analysis, causation evaluation, and litigation focused clinical reasoning.

Importantly, the Lexcura Clinical Intelligence Model™ is built upon analytical discipline rather than predetermined conclusions. Strong analysis requires restraint, physiologic coherence, evidentiary support, and reasoning that remains stable when the progression is examined more closely.

Healthcare systems continue becoming more operationally and clinically complex, and medical-legal analysis must evolve accordingly.

My hope is that this framework contributes to a more organized, disciplined, and clinically grounded approach to medical-legal evaluation for attorneys, clinicians, consultants, and healthcare professionals working within increasingly complex litigation environments.

Founder & Chief Clinical Strategist

Lexcura Summit

TABLE OF CONTENTS

CHAPTER - 01

RECORD INTEGRITY

Before causation can be evaluated, the records must first establish reality.

This chapter establishes a foundational pillar within the Lexcura Clinical Intelligence Model™ creating the evidentiary framework required for defensible medical-legal analysis.

THE PURPOSE OF THIS PILLAR

Record Integrity establishes whether the medical record can support a stable reconstruction of the clinical sequence itself. Before breach, causation, litigation exposure, or case value can be evaluated responsibly, the chronology must first demonstrate sufficient continuity, sequencing stability, escalation visibility, and documentation reliability to support meaningful analysis.

This pillar examines how documentation integrity shapes defensibility by determining whether deterioration, intervention opportunity, provider awareness, physiologic progression, and clinical decision-making can be reconstructed with confidence. It also explores how unstable records gradually weaken causation analysis, increase interpretive vulnerability, and undermine the structural stability of the litigation itself.

Because within the Lexcura Clinical Intelligence Model™, every later analytical conclusion depends upon whether the underlying records can first establish a reliable clinical foundation.

Why This Pillar Comes First

Before causation can be analyzed, before breach can be evaluated, and before litigation value can be assessed, the records themselves must first establish whether reality can be reconstructed with sufficient confidence.

This is why the Lexcura Clinical Intelligence Model™ begins with Record Integrity. Because every later analytical conclusion depends upon the stability of the underlying documentation.

If the records cannot establish clinical sequencing, reliable escalation visibility, intervention timing, and logical progression of deterioration, then every downstream pillar becomes increasingly vulnerable. Baseline analysis weakens when the timeline can no longer be established reliably. Standard of care interpretation becomes increasingly subjective. Causation shifts away from evidence-based reasoning and toward speculation.

Attorneys often focus first on catastrophic injury, emotional impact, apparent delay, or potential damages. Yet many cases that initially appear powerful begin to collapse once the records are tested for analytical reliability.

The strength of litigation is not determined solely by what allegedly occurred.

It is determined by whether the records can reliably establish what occurred. That distinction forms the foundation of the entire model.

Because before an attorney can determine whether an outcome was altered by a deviation in care, another question must first be answered:

Can the underlying reality of the case actually be reconstructed with confidence? Everything else depends upon that answer.

Defining Record Integrity

Within the Lexcura Clinical Intelligence Model™, Record Integrity refers to the reliability, continuity, consistency, and coherence of the medical documentation itself. It is not simply a question of whether records exist, but whether the records can establish reliable reconstruction of what actually occurred.

In strong cases, the documentation allows deterioration, intervention timing, escalation pathways, and clinical reasoning to be followed with confidence. The records create a cohesive clinical narrative capable of withstanding scrutiny.

In weak cases, the experience is very different. The reviewer encounters conflicting timestamps, incomplete reassessments, missing escalation documentation, and unexplained gaps during critical periods of deterioration. As the documentation becomes less stable, confidence in the analysis weakens with it.

An attorney may initially believe the matter is highly compelling because the injury appears catastrophic and the alleged delay seems obvious on preliminary review. Yet as instability within the records emerges, questions that initially appeared answerable become increasingly uncertain. When did deterioration become identifiable? When should escalation reasonably have occurred? Could the outcome realistically have been altered given the patient's underlying physiology?

In many cases, these questions cannot be answered confidently because the records no longer support stable reconstruction.

Importantly, Record Integrity is not determined by the volume of documentation alone. Thousands of pages of records may still produce unstable litigation if reassessment patterns remain incomplete, escalation documentation conflicts between providers, or critical periods of deterioration are missing entirely.

A defining truth of medical litigation is that the reliability of the analysis can never exceed the reliability of the records upon which the analysis depends.

The Foundation of Every Defensible Case

At intake, the case appeared compelling.

A 58-year-old patient presented to the emergency department with chest pain, shortness of breath, diaphoresis, and progressive instability. Hours later, the patient suffered a significant myocardial infarction resulting in permanent cardiac impairment.

The allegations initially appeared straightforward. The injuries were substantial, the timeline appeared concerning, and the potential damages were significant. The family believed the outcome should have been preventable. The attorney identified possible delay in escalation and intervention.

But within days of structured analysis, the case began to weaken rapidly.

Not because the outcome was insignificant. Not because the care was necessarily appropriate. And not because there was no potential deviation in treatment.

The case weakened because the records could no longer support a reliable reconstruction of what had actually occurred.

Critical nursing documentation was missing. Medication administration records contained timing inconsistencies. Escalation documentation conflicted between providers, and unexplained gaps emerged during the most important period of deterioration.

As the records became less stable, every downstream analytical conclusion weakened with them. Standard of care analysis became increasingly interpretive. Causation shifted away from evidence-based reconstruction and toward speculation.

Eventually, the central issue was no longer whether something may have gone wrong. The more important question became whether it could ever be proven.

Because medical litigation is not built upon allegation alone. It is built upon the ability to reconstruct, analyze, and defend what actually occurred using records capable of surviving scrutiny.

That process begins with Record Integrity.

The Foundation Of The Entire Model

Every analytical conclusion within the Lexcura Clinical Intelligence Model™ depends upon the reliability of the underlying records. When documentation becomes unstable, baseline physiology becomes more difficult to establish, visibility into clinical reasoning weakens, and causation grows increasingly vulnerable to speculation rather than evidence-based analysis.

For this reason, Record Integrity is not simply an intake function or organizational process within the model. It is the analytical foundation upon which every later conclusion depends. If the records cannot sustain reliable documentation continuity, the entire litigation framework becomes unstable regardless of how severe the outcome may initially appear.

Attorneys are naturally drawn toward catastrophic injury, apparent delay, and emotional impact early in litigation. Yet many cases that initially appear compelling begin to weaken once the underlying documentation is tested under scrutiny.

Severe injury alone does not create defensible litigation. Before a case can be evaluated responsibly, the records must first support reliable analysis.

If they cannot, every later conclusion becomes increasingly vulnerable.

When Outcome Creates False Confidence

One of the most common mistakes in medical litigation is allowing the severity of the outcome to create premature confidence in causation before the underlying documentation has been tested for structural strength.

Catastrophic injuries naturally draw attention toward damages, emotional impact, and apparent treatment delay. Attorneys may initially believe the case is highly defensible because the outcome itself appears so severe. However, early confidence built primarily upon injury magnitude can become dangerously misleading when the records are later examined in detail.

In some cases, the attorney may already have invested months into the litigation before the chronology begins to destabilize and the underlying evidentiary weaknesses become fully visible.

Many cases begin weakening long before causation is formally analyzed.

It begins when the records fail to establish continuity, clear escalation timing, clear clinical progression, or meaningful intervention opportunity. Once those elements become unstable, every later analytical conclusion becomes increasingly vulnerable regardless of how compelling the injury may appear emotionally.

A central reason the Lexcura Clinical Intelligence Model™ begins with Record Integrity rather than breach analysis or damages evaluation is its recognition that all subsequent reasoning depends on the stability of the underlying record.

Because before an attorney can determine whether a deviation probably altered outcome, the records must first establish whether the timeline itself can be reconstructed reliably enough to support reliable analysis.

Without that foundation, litigation strategy can become anchored to assumption rather than evidence.

And in medical litigation, assumption is rarely sustainable for long.

An attorney may spend months building what initially appears to be a highly compelling sepsis case, only to discover during expert review that critical reassessment documentation is missing during the most determinative period of deterioration. By the time the instability within the chronology becomes fully apparent, substantial litigation resources may already have been invested and settlement expectations may already be anchored to assumptions the records ultimately cannot support.

The Difference Between Documentation And Clinical Reality

One of the foundational concepts in medical litigation is understanding that the medical record is not the clinical event itself.

It is the reconstruction of the event.

Healthcare providers experience patient deterioration in real time through evolving assessment, communication, observation, clinical judgment, and ongoing decision making. Litigation, however, does not evaluate memory or retrospective explanation. It evaluates what the records can demonstrate under scrutiny.

That distinction fundamentally alters the defensibility of the entire litigation analysis.

Care may have occurred appropriately. Escalation discussions may have taken place.

Concerns may have been recognized. Clinical reasoning may have existed. Providers may remember exactly why decisions were made and what they believed at the time.

An ICU nurse may later testify that the physician was notified repeatedly as the patient deteriorated. The physician may fully agree that escalation discussions occurred. Yet if the documentation contains no visible escalation pathway, no time stamped communication, and no reassessment sequence supporting that testimony, the litigation analysis may treat the escalation as though it never occurred at all.

Among the harshest realities in medical litigation is this:

If you didn't write it down, legally, it may be treated as though it never happened.

That single principle can determine whether an otherwise stable case remains defensible under scrutiny.

Litigation does not evaluate what clinicians remember.
It evaluates what the records can prove.

Information Does Not Equal Defensibility

One of the most common misconceptions in medical - legal review is assuming that large volumes of documentation automatically create analytical strength. They do not.

Thousands of pages of records may still produce an unreliable dataset if the information lacks continuity, internal consistency, documentation continuity, or visibility into clinical reasoning.

A record set filled with fragmented assessments, repetitive charting, conflicting timestamps, retrospective entries, or missing escalation documentation may initially appear comprehensive while actually weakening the litigation analysis substantially.

This creates what may best be described as false stability. The records appear extensive, the chart appears organized, and the sheer volume of documentation creates the illusion of analytical security. Yet beneath the surface, the integrity required for stable sequencing may still be missing entirely.

This is where many cases quietly begin to deteriorate - not because the reviewer lacks intelligence or experience, but because the integrity of the underlying information was never properly evaluated before deeper conclusions were formed.

In litigation, information alone does not create stability. Chronology does.

Clinical Intelligence Warning

A chronology that cannot sustain timeline reconstruction may still create the illusion of strong causation.

Among the most dangerous forms of analytical instability in medical litigation is the tendency for catastrophic injury to psychologically obscure evidentiary weakness.

Attorneys, experts, and even experienced reviewers may initially believe a case appears highly substantiated simply because the outcome itself is severe and the alleged delay appears compelling at first review.

Yet severe outcomes do not automatically establish defensible causation.

As chronology becomes fragmented, escalation visibility weakens, intervention timing grows uncertain, and documentation gaps disrupt evidence-based chronology, the analytical foundation beneath the litigation may already be deteriorating long before causation is formally evaluated.

This is why emotionally compelling cases often require the most disciplined Record Integrity analysis.

Because in medical litigation, the appearance of causation strength and the ability to prove causation are not always the same thing.

The Hidden Danger Of Missing Time

Most catastrophic litigation cases ultimately revolve around timing.

The critical issue is often not simply what occurred, but when deterioration began, when escalation became necessary, when intervention opportunity narrowed, and whether meaningful reversibility still existed at the time of the alleged deviation.

When those moments cannot be reconstructed reliably, the entire case becomes vulnerable regardless of how severe the outcome may appear.

A missing thirty-minute documentation window in a sepsis case may determine whether causation survives. An undocumented medication administration time may eliminate the ability to establish meaningful treatment delay. A gap in neurological reassessments may destroy the ability to demonstrate deterioration entirely.

These are not minor documentation inconveniences. They are analytical failures with the potential to destabilize the litigation structure at its core. Because in medical litigation, timing is not simply part of the analysis.

Timing often determines the analysis.

In many cases, the most damaging documentation gap is not hours long. Sometimes the entire direction of causation analysis changes because of twenty undocumented minutes during active deterioration. The attorney may initially view the delay as obvious, only to later discover that the precise moment of physiologic decline can no longer be established with confidence.

> *Framework Principle*
>
> In medical litigation, timing is not simply part of the analysis. Timing often determines the analysis.

Record Integrity And Causation

Causation is often discussed as though it exists independently from the records. In reality, causation can only be established through defensible reconstruction of the patient's condition, deterioration, intervention timing, and course of events. When documentation becomes unstable, analysis gradually shifts away from evidence based reasoning and toward interpretation and assumption.

In medical litigation, causation is not built on speculation. It is built on chronology, timing, physiology, and evidence-based reconstruction.

This is why Record Integrity determines whether litigation analysis remains evidence based or becomes increasingly vulnerable to assumption.

The Danger Of Retrospective Reconstruction

One of the greatest risks in litigation analysis is retrospective assumption.

When documentation gaps exist, reviewers may unintentionally infer sequence, assume escalation occurred, fill missing timelines, or reconstruct undocumented events based upon later outcomes. This becomes especially dangerous in catastrophic cases where hindsight naturally creates pressure to believe deterioration should have been recognized earlier.

But assumptions inserted into missing documentation create analytical instability.

The more gaps that exist within the records, the more vulnerable the analysis becomes to challenge under scrutiny.

Strong litigation analysis does not assume what probably occurred.

It establishes what can actually be demonstrated reliably from the records themselves.

That distinction is critical because medicine is practiced prospectively, while litigation evaluates events retrospectively. Without reliable documentation anchoring the sequence of events, retrospective interpretation can easily distort what was actually identifiable to clinicians at the time care was delivered.

Documentation Failure vs Clinical Failure

Another important distinction must be understood.

Poor documentation does not automatically mean poor clinical care occurred. In many cases, clinicians may have acted reasonably in real time while failing to document the reasoning, reassessment, or escalation pathway clearly enough for litigation review years later. And poor clinical care does not always produce poor documentation.

Sometimes both exist simultaneously. In other cases, however, the documentation itself becomes the central vulnerability regardless of whether the care may have been reasonable.

This is particularly important because documentation failure alone may weaken defensibility, damage provider credibility, destabilize expert analysis, and significantly increase litigation exposure.

The inability to demonstrate clinical reasoning can become nearly as damaging as the underlying allegation itself.

Because once visibility into decision-making disappears, retrospective criticism becomes substantially easier.

This reality is frequently underestimated by both clinicians and attorneys. In many cases, the records themselves become the battlefield upon which litigation strength is ultimately determined.

Why Weak Records Make Experts Vulnerable

Weak records do not only weaken the case.

They also weaken the expert opinions built upon the chronology itself.

When documentation gaps prevent reconstruction, opinions become increasingly interpretive, assumptions become more visible, and causation becomes substantially more vulnerable to attack.

Experts who initially expressed confidence in the case may become increasingly cautious as sequencing gaps emerge and the chronology becomes more difficult to defend with certainty.

Experts who overstate certainty within unstable records often become highly exposed during deposition and cross-examination because the foundation supporting their conclusions may not actually exist within the documentation itself.

A key reason the Lexcura Clinical Intelligence Model™ places such substantial emphasis on Record Integrity is to ensure that deeper analytical conclusions are grounded in reliable documentation.

Strong expert testimony requires stable chronology, reliable escalation visibility, reliable intervention timing, and reliable physiologic reconstruction. Without those elements, even highly experienced experts may struggle to sustain credible opinions under scrutiny.

An expert may initially express strong confidence during early review, only to become progressively more cautious once conflicting timestamps, missing reassessments, and unstable chronology begin to emerge during deposition preparation. In many cases, the weakness is not the expert's reasoning itself, but the instability of the documentation supporting the opinion.

Record Integrity Is Analytical Infrastructure

One of the greatest misconceptions surrounding record review is believing that it is primarily administrative rather than analytical.

Record Integrity is analytical infrastructure.

Every downstream pillar depends upon whether the records can support coherent reconstruction. Once documentation becomes unstable, chronology weakens, clinical reasoning becomes less visible, and causation grows increasingly vulnerable to speculation.

This is why Record Integrity serves as the gateway to the Lexcura Clinical Intelligence Model™. Without it, every later analytical conclusion becomes less reliable.

Clinical Intelligence Insight

Attorneys often focus first on breach, damages, or emotional impact because those elements appear most visible at intake. Yet the long-term stability of the case is often determined much earlier - at the point where the records either establish or fail to establish a reliable course of events.

This is why Record Integrity functions as the gateway to every later pillar within the Lexcura Clinical Intelligence Model™. Once chronology becomes unstable, escalation analysis grows increasingly interpretive and causation becomes progressively more vulnerable to challenge.

An attorney may initially focus on the severity of the injury while overlooking subtle instability within the records themselves. Months later, during expert review or deposition preparation, the litigation strategy may begin to weaken once the chronology can no longer support causation with confidence.

Strong litigation strategy begins with reliable reconstruction.
And reliable reconstruction begins with Record Integrity.

The Strategic Importance Of Strong Records

Importantly, strong records do not automatically favor one side of litigation.

In some cases, highly detailed documentation may strengthen plaintiff arguments by clearly establishing delayed escalation, missed intervention opportunity, or visible deterioration unfolding. In other cases, strong documentation may significantly strengthen the defense by demonstrating repeated reassessment, timely escalation, active clinical reasoning, and consistent intervention efforts.

This is an important principle within the Lexcura Clinical Intelligence Model™: Record Integrity is neutral infrastructure.

It strengthens whichever position the records themselves can reliably support.

That neutrality is critical because defensible litigation analysis cannot begin from predetermined conclusions.

It must begin from a substantiated chronology.

The Attorney's Analytical Obligation

Attorneys often begin litigation by focusing on breach, damages, or emotional impact. But before those issues can be evaluated responsibly, another issue must first be resolved:

Can the timeline be reconstructed with confidence?

Because if the records cannot establish timing, progression, escalation, intervention opportunity, and clinical reasoning reliably, the litigation strategy itself becomes unstable.

Cases do not collapse solely because care was appropriate.

Many collapse because the records cannot sustain justifiable proof of what actually occurred. That distinction changes the entire approach to litigation analysis.

> *Framework Principle*
> Before breach can be analyzed responsibly, reality itself must first be reconstructable. Record Integrity is not simply the first pillar of the Lexcura Clinical Intelligence Model™.

It is the evidentiary foundation upon which every later analytical conclusion depends. It determines whether litigation analysis remains evidence-based or assumption based.

Without reliable records, timelines weaken, causation unravels, expert credibility becomes vulnerable, and litigation strategy becomes increasingly speculative.

This is why the model begins here.

Because before an attorney can determine whether a deviation altered outcome, another question must first be answered:

Can reality itself be reconstructed reliably enough to survive scrutiny? Everything else depends upon that answer.

Strong litigation is not built solely on severe outcomes.

It is built on records capable of supporting coherent reconstruction.

Because in medical litigation, the strength of the case depends not only on what happened...

but on whether it can actually be proven.

Applying Record Integrity In Litigation Analysis

Understanding the principles of Record Integrity conceptually is only the beginning. The true importance of this pillar becomes apparent when the framework is applied within actual litigation analysis.

In practice, Record Integrity determines whether deterioration, escalation timing, intervention opportunity, and causation can be evaluated with confidence. The following examples demonstrate how documentation quality can dramatically alter the direction of a case even when the underlying injuries appear severe.

In some matters, reliable records support clear analysis of escalation and intervention timing. In others, incomplete or inconsistent documentation makes it difficult to determine whether the alleged deviation materially altered the patient's outcome.

These examples reinforce one of the central principles of the Lexcura Clinical Intelligence Model™: Litigation strength is determined not only by what happened, but by whether the records can reliably prove what happened.

CASE ANALYSIS - 1

Stable Chronology Supporting Sustainable Causation

A 46-year-old male presented to the emergency department with chest pain, diaphoresis, nausea, and progressive shortness of breath. Initial nursing documentation was completed promptly and included detailed symptom assessment, complete vital signs, clearly documented cardiac risk factors, and precise time stamped escalation notes. An electrocardiogram demonstrated evolving ischemic changes, and serial troponin testing was initiated according to protocol.

Over the next several hours, the records demonstrated progressive symptom escalation, repeated reassessments, physician notification, cardiology consultation, and eventual transfer for intervention. Despite these actions, the documentation also established a clearly identifiable two-hour delay between recognition of evolving instability and activation of definitive cardiac intervention.

At first review, the case appeared highly compelling from a plaintiff perspective. The records demonstrated a visible unfolding of deterioration, a measurable intervention delay, and a sequence of escalating clinical findings that could be reconstructed with unusual clarity.

More importantly, the chronology remained internally consistent throughout the flow of care.

The records established when deterioration first became identifiable, when escalation thresholds were reached, when providers became aware of the patient's instability, what interventions were performed, and precisely where delays occurred within the treatment sequence.

This distinction significantly strengthened the overall stability of the case.

An attorney reviewing the matter would not be forced to rely heavily upon assumption, retrospective interpretation, or conflicting reconstruction. Instead, the chronology itself created a stable analytical foundation capable of supporting expert analysis, causation evaluation, and litigation strategy with a high degree of confidence.

Because the records were complete, properly sequenced, and supported by objective clinical findings, Baseline Profiling could establish that the patient possessed meaningful physiologic reserve and substantial recovery potential prior to the event.

Timeline Reconstruction could identify the intervention window with relative precision. Standard of Care Review could evaluate escalation obligations against a reconstruction rather than fragmented documentation.

Primarily, Causation Mapping could evaluate whether earlier intervention would probably have altered the severity of the patient's myocardial damage without relying primarily upon retrospective inference.

That distinction fundamentally changes the sustainability of causation analysis.

An expert reviewing this case would be able to explain not only that deterioration occurred, but when it became recognizable, when escalation obligations were triggered, how long intervention opportunity remained available, and why the documented delay may have materially altered the patient's outcome.

This is the strategic importance of Record Integrity.

When chronology remains stable, expert opinions become more durable because the timeline can withstand scrutiny. Escalation timing becomes defensible because intervention opportunity can be identified clearly. Causation analysis becomes more sustainable because the progression of deterioration can be reconstructed directly from the records rather than inferred retrospectively months or years later during litigation.

As a result, litigation strategy itself becomes significantly more stable.

The strength of the case did not arise solely from the severity of the injury. It arose from the ability to reconstruct the course of events, escalation opportunity, intervention delay, and physiologic impact through documentation capable of sustaining scrutiny.

These are the pivotal distinctions in medical litigation. Strong cases are not built solely on catastrophic outcomes.

They are built on records capable of proving what actually happened.

CASE ANALYSIS - 2

Litigation Destabilization Following Record Integrity Failure

An 82-year-old female with advanced heart failure, chronic kidney disease, diabetes, and significant frailty presented to a long-term care facility with worsening confusion, hypotension, and progressive respiratory decline. Within twenty-four hours, the patient developed septic shock and was transferred emergently to the hospital, where she later died.

At intake, the case appeared highly concerning.

The family alleged delayed recognition of deterioration, failure to escalate appropriately, delayed physician notification, and failure to transfer the patient to a higher level of care in a timely manner. The outcome was catastrophic, emotionally compelling, and initially appeared to create substantial liability exposure.

Early review suggested the case might involve significant failures in escalation and intervention timing.

However, once the records underwent structured integrity analysis, the case began to weaken rapidly.

Critical nursing documentation was missing during the primary period of deterioration. Vital sign recordings were incomplete and inconsistent between shifts. Several entries appeared to have been retrospectively documented, making sequencing unreliable. Escalation documentation conflicted between providers, and medication administration records contained significant timing gaps.

As reconstruction became more difficult, the central issue in the case began to shift. The question was no longer simply whether deterioration had occurred.

The question became whether the records could establish with confidence when the deterioration became identifiable, when escalation obligations were triggered, and whether meaningful intervention opportunity still existed at the time of the alleged delay.

That distinction ultimately became fatal to the litigation analysis.

Without precise sequencing, it was no longer clear when escalation should reasonably have occurred, when physician notification became necessary, whether meaningful intervention opportunity remained available, or whether earlier transfer would probably have altered the patient's trajectory in any measurable way.

As the records became less reliable, every downstream analytical pillar began weakening with them.

Baseline Profiling demonstrated profound pre-existing physiologic compromise and extremely limited reserve. Timeline Reconstruction could not establish a reliable sequence of deterioration or escalation opportunity. Standard of Care Review became increasingly interpretive because the documentation failed to establish what providers actually knew at critical moments during the patient's sequencing. Ultimately, the greatest instability emerged within Causation Mapping.

Because no credible intervention window could be established reliably, the analysis became increasingly speculative. While it remained possible that earlier intervention may have altered some aspect of the patient's progression, the records could not support causation with the level of certainty required to sustain the case.

When fully evaluated, the more important issue became whether the records could prove that the alleged failures probably changed the outcome.

Ultimately, the records could not support that conclusion with enough certainty to sustain defensible causation.

As a result, the case gradually lost causation stability, expert confidence, litigation leverage, and overall strategic value.

As the analytical foundation weakened, settlement posture may also have shifted substantially because the ability to sustain defensible causation became increasingly uncertain.

The catastrophic outcome itself remained emotionally compelling. However, the inability to reconstruct the timeline reliably prevented the case from sustaining evidence-based causation analysis under scrutiny.

Severe injury alone does not create a viable case.

A structured causation analysis is what achieves that outcome.

Without reliable records, timing becomes uncertain, escalation becomes increasingly interpretive, and causation becomes vulnerable to attack.

This is why Record Integrity is not merely an intake function within the Lexcura Clinical Intelligence Model™.

It is the structural foundation upon which every later analytical conclusion depends. Many cases do not collapse because no deviation occurred.

They collapse because the records cannot prove whether the deviation materially changed the outcome.

READER EXERCISE

Applying Record Integrity Analysis

Understanding Record Integrity conceptually is very different from applying it within active litigation analysis.

In practice, attorneys and experts are rarely evaluating perfect records. More commonly, they are forced to determine whether incomplete, inconsistent, or unstable documentation can still support progression of deterioration, escalation opportunity, intervention timing, and causation.

This distinction is critical because within the Lexcura Clinical Intelligence Model™, the central issue is not simply whether a deviation may have occurred. The central issue is whether the records can reliably establish what occurred, when it occurred, and whether the alleged failure probably altered the patient's trajectory.

The following scenario is designed to mirror the type of instability frequently encountered during real litigation review.

As you work through the case, approach the records as though you are evaluating an actual intake matter. Resist the temptation to focus solely on the severity of the outcome. Instead, evaluate whether the documentation itself can sustain continuity within the records of the course of events.

That distinction forms the analytical foundation upon which every later pillar of the model depends.

Evaluating Record Integrity and Litigation Stability

A 71-year-old male with chronic obstructive pulmonary disease, congestive heart failure, diabetes, and chronic kidney disease presented to the emergency department with worsening shortness of breath, confusion, and hypotension.

The patient was admitted with suspected sepsis. Approximately twelve hours later, he suffered respiratory collapse requiring intubation and ICU transfer. He later developed multi-organ failure and died several days afterward.

The family alleges delayed recognition of deterioration, failure to escalate appropriately, delayed physician notification, and delayed initiation of sepsis treatment.

At intake, the case initially appears significant. The outcome is catastrophic, the allegations involve potential delay in escalation, and the progression toward respiratory collapse creates the appearance of substantial causation exposure.

However, during structured review, several documentation concerns begin to emerge.

Nursing reassessment documentation is missing for a three-hour period during reported deterioration. Medication administration records contain inconsistent timestamps, and physician notification times differ between nursing notes and provider documentation.

One progress note appears duplicated from an earlier entry despite clear evidence that the patient's condition had changed substantially during that period.

Vital signs were also recorded inconsistently, and no clear documentation establishes when the patient first met sepsis escalation criteria.

As the integrity of the records becomes less stable, the central litigation question begins to shift.

The issue is no longer simply whether deterioration occurred.

The litigation focus becomes whether the records can establish when deterioration became identifiable, when escalation obligations were triggered, whether meaningful intervention opportunity still existed, and whether earlier intervention would probably have altered the patient's outcome.

Using the principles of the Lexcura Clinical Intelligence Model™, evaluate whether the records can support a structured and defensible chronology.

Litigation Analysis Application

1. Initial Structural Defensibility Concerns

At first review, what aspects of the documentation create the greatest concern regarding Record Integrity?

Consider whether the records provide sufficient continuity, sequencing reliability, escalation visibility, and documentation consistency to support stable litigation analysis.

2. Reliability of Timeline Reconstruction

Can the sequence of deterioration and escalation be built with reasonable confidence?

If not, identify the specific documentation failures that destabilize the chronology.

3. Impact on Standard of Care Analysis

How do documentation inconsistencies affect the ability to evaluate recognition of deterioration, escalation timing, physician awareness, and intervention opportunity? At what point does Standard of Care Review begin shifting away from evidence based analysis and toward interpretive reconstruction due to instability within the chronology itself?

4. Impact on Causation Stability

How does the instability of the records affect the ability to establish whether earlier intervention would probably have altered the patient's trajectory? Can meaningful reversibility still be evaluated reliably from the documentation available?

5. *Litigation Sustainability Assessment*

Based upon the documentation currently available, how would you characterize the overall sustainability of the case? Does the matter appear structurally stable, moderately vulnerable, or increasingly speculative as the chronology becomes less reliable? Of greatest significance, explain which documentation failures most significantly weaken the ability to sustain defensible causation and litigation strategy.

Answer Key & Analysis

The primary weakness in this case is not necessarily the severity of the outcome itself, but the instability of the underlying documentation.

At intake, the matter appears highly concerning because the patient experienced catastrophic deterioration following suspected sepsis. However, once the records undergo structured integrity analysis, significant instability begins to emerge within the chronology itself.

The missing reassessment period during deterioration creates substantial uncertainty regarding when the patient's condition became clearly unstable, when escalation obligations should reasonably have been triggered, and whether meaningful intervention opportunity remained available at the time of the alleged delay.

The conflicting timestamps further weaken sequencing reliability. Because physician notification timing cannot be established confidently, Standard of Care Review gradually shifts away from evidence-based reconstruction and toward interpretive analysis.

That distinction is critical.

Once chronology becomes unstable, every downstream analytical pillar begins weakening with it.

Timeline reconstruction can no longer establish deterioration progression reliably. Causation Mapping becomes increasingly speculative because intervention opportunity cannot be identified with confidence.

Baseline Profiling also becomes highly significant because the patient already possessed substantial physiologic compromise prior to the event, limiting reserve and reducing certainty regarding reversibility.

As a result, the case becomes progressively more vulnerable from a litigation perspective. This does not necessarily mean no deviation occurred.

It means the records may be incapable of proving when the deviation occurred, whether meaningful intervention opportunity still existed, and whether the alleged delay probably altered the outcome.

That distinction lies at the center of Record Integrity analysis.

Key Teaching Point

The strength of litigation is determined not only by what happened, but by whether the records can sustain defensible analysis of what actually occurred.

Without stable reconstruction, timelines weaken, breach analysis becomes unstable, and causation becomes increasingly speculative.

That is why Record Integrity forms the foundation of the entire Lexcura Clinical Intelligence Model™.

Chapter 1 Takeaways

Record Integrity

1. Record Integrity determines whether litigation remains evidence-based or becomes interpretive.

When documentation continuity weakens, analysis gradually shifts away from stable reconstruction and toward inference, assumption, and speculation.

2. Severe outcomes alone do not create sustainable causation.

Emotional impact and catastrophic injury may initially strengthen the appearance of the case, but defensible litigation depends upon whether the records can establish that the alleged failure probably altered the patient's outcome.

3. The medical record is not the clinical event itself.

It is the reconstruction of the event. Litigation evaluates what can be demonstrated within the documentation - not what providers later remember, intended, or believed occurred.

4. Missing time erodes causation.

When deterioration, escalation opportunity, intervention timing, or course of events cannot be reconstructed coherently, the analytical foundation of the case begins to weaken rapidly.

5. Weak records weaken both the case and the expert.

Experts depend upon reliable chronology, visible escalation pathways, and stable reconstruction. Once documentation gaps disrupt that foundation, expert opinions become increasingly vulnerable under scrutiny.

6. Documentation failure can independently increase litigation exposure.

Poor documentation does not automatically establish poor clinical care. However, once reassessment visibility, escalation reasoning, and clinical decision-making disappear from the records, retrospective criticism becomes substantially easier.

7. Strong records are neutral analytical infrastructure.

Reliable documentation may strengthen either plaintiff or defense positioning depending upon what the records actually demonstrate. Record Integrity exists to support evidence-based analysis - not predetermined conclusions.

8. Information volume does not equal analytical strength.

Thousands of pages of documentation may still produce unstable litigation if continuity, reassessment patterns, escalation visibility, and chronology remain fragmented or inconsistent.

9. *Every analytical pillar depends upon Record Integrity.*

Baseline Profiling, Timeline Reconstruction, Standard of Care Review, Regulatory Analysis, and Causation Mapping all rely upon whether the underlying records can sustain defensible reconstruction.

10. *Before causation can be analyzed responsibly, the records must first establish what actually occurred.*

Before breach, damages, or litigation value can be evaluated responsibly, the records must first establish what actually occurred. Without that foundation, every later conclusion becomes progressively more vulnerable.

Transition To The Next Pillar

Once Record Integrity establishes whether the chronology remains sufficiently stable, the next question becomes equally important: even if the timeline can be reconstructed reliably, was the patient physiologically capable of meaningful recovery in the first place?

Chronology alone does not establish causation. A delayed intervention does not carry the same litigation significance in every patient because the effect of timing, escalation, and treatment opportunity is profoundly influenced by the patient's baseline physiology long before the alleged deviation ever occurred.

Two patients may experience the same delay in treatment yet possess entirely different litigation trajectories depending upon their physiologic reserve, comorbid burden, functional impairment, frailty, and overall recovery potential.

In some patients, earlier intervention may have created a meaningful opportunity to alter outcome severity. In others, advanced physiologic compromise may have limited reversibility long before the alleged deviation took place.

This is where Baseline Profiling becomes critical.

Before causation can be evaluated responsibly, the patient's pre-existing physiologic condition must first be understood within the context of resilience, reversibility, and probable recovery trajectory. Without that foundation, even well-documented timelines and clearly established escalation delays may create a misleading impression of causation strength.

In many cases, the most significant litigation question is not simply whether deterioration occurred. The more important question is whether the patient possessed meaningful physiologic capacity for recovery at the time intervention opportunity still existed.

The next pillar examines how baseline health status influences intervention opportunity, reversibility, causation probability, litigation strength, and ultimately case value itself.

Because in medical litigation, physiology defines possibility long before causation is ever analyzed.

And before timing can alter outcome, the patient must first possess the physiologic capacity for outcome to be altered at all.

The strength of litigation is ultimately determined not by allegation alone, but by whether the clinical truth can still be reconstructed from the records left behind.

The Lexcura
Clinical Intelligence Model™

"Before causation can be evaluated responsibly, the records must first establish what happened and the patient's baseline must reveal what was still physiologically possible."

CHAPTER - 02

BASELINE PROFILING

Establishing the patient's physiologic starting point.

This chapter establishes a foundational pillar within the Lexcura Clinical Intelligence Model™ creating the evidentiary framework required for defensible medical-legal analysis.

DEFINING POSSIBILITY BEFORE CAUSATION

At intake, the case appeared devastating.

An 84-year-old female resident of a skilled nursing facility developed progressive respiratory distress, worsening confusion, hypotension, and declining oxygen saturation over the course of several hours. Staff documentation reflected delayed physician notification, inconsistent reassessment intervals, and a late transfer to the emergency department. Within twenty-four hours of hospital admission, the patient required intubation for septic shock and multi-organ failure. She died three days later.

The family believed the outcome should have been preventable. The attorney initially agreed.

The records appeared to demonstrate visible deterioration, delayed escalation, and possible missed intervention opportunity. Early review suggested the matter could represent a significant failure in sepsis recognition and timely transfer.

But as the analysis progressed, the case began shifting in a very different direction.

Not because the documentation was weak. In many respects, the records were relatively strong. The chronology could be reconstructed with reasonable confidence. Escalation timing could be evaluated. Intervention windows could be identified.

The deeper issue emerged elsewhere.

The patient's baseline physiology revealed profound pre-existing compromise long before the alleged deviation ever occurred.

She suffered from advanced congestive heart failure, severe chronic kidney disease, insulin-dependent diabetes, chronic malnutrition, recurrent aspiration pneumonia, progressive frailty, and substantial functional decline. Multiple admissions over the previous year demonstrated steadily worsening physiologic reserve. Several specialists had already documented poor long-term prognosis and limited recovery potential even before the final hospitalization.

The central analytical question gradually changed.

The issue was no longer simply whether deterioration occurred or whether escalation should have happened earlier.

The more important question became whether meaningful recovery had ever been physiologically possible in the first place.

That distinction forms the foundation of Baseline Profiling within the Lexcura Clinical Intelligence Model™.

Because in medical litigation, chronology alone does not establish causation. Physiology determines possibility.

And before timing can alter outcome, the patient must first possess sufficient physiologic reserve for outcome to be realistically alterable at all.

Defining Baseline Profiling

Within the Lexcura Clinical Intelligence Model™, Baseline Profiling refers to the structured evaluation of the patient's pre-existing physiologic condition before the alleged deviation occurred. This includes analysis of comorbid burden, frailty, functional status, prior deterioration patterns, recovery potential, chronic disease progression, and overall physiologic reserve.

The purpose of Baseline Profiling is not simply to identify medical diagnoses. It is to determine the degree to which the patient possessed meaningful capacity for reversibility before the event being litigated.

This shift becomes central to litigation strategy because two patients may experience the same delay in treatment yet possess entirely different litigation trajectories depending upon their underlying physiology.

A previously healthy 42-year-old with strong reserve may possess substantial capacity for recovery even after delayed intervention. An 89-year-old patient with advanced dementia, severe heart failure, chronic malnutrition, and progressive multi-organ compromise may possess extremely limited reversibility long before the alleged delay ever occurred.

The delay itself may appear similar.

The physiologic meaning of the delay may be profoundly different.

This is why Baseline Profiling serves as one of the central analytical pillars of the model. Because before causation can be evaluated responsibly, possibility must first be defined.

The Difference Between Injury And Reversibility

One of the most common misconceptions in medical litigation is assuming that severe injury automatically implies preventability.

It does not.

Catastrophic outcomes are emotionally powerful. They naturally create retrospective pressure to believe that earlier intervention should have changed the trajectory.

Families often experience this belief intensely because deterioration appears sudden, dramatic, and deeply personal. Attorneys may initially experience the same reaction when reviewing cases involving death, paralysis, amputation, neurologic injury, or permanent disability.

But severe outcome alone does not establish that meaningful reversibility existed. This distinction is one of the most important concepts within Baseline Profiling.

Medicine does not operate within theoretical possibility alone. It operates within physiologic limitation.

Some patients possess substantial reserve capable of tolerating delayed intervention while still maintaining recovery potential. Others possess so little reserve that even appropriate intervention may carry limited probability of altering outcome meaningfully. In litigation, this divide fundamentally changes causation analysis.

Because causation is not determined solely by whether deterioration occurred.

It is determined by whether the patient's physiology realistically allowed the outcome to be altered at the time intervention opportunity still existed.

Why Frailty Changes Litigation Analysis

Frailty is often underestimated in medical litigation because it may not appear as dramatic or visible as acute injury. Yet in many cases, frailty influences causation analysis more than the alleged deviation itself.

A frail patient may already possess severely limited reserve long before the critical event occurs. Cardiac compensation may be diminished. Pulmonary tolerance may already be impaired. Nutritional decline, chronic illness, reduced mobility, recurrent admissions, and progressive functional deterioration may all substantially limit recovery potential even before the alleged delay takes place.

These distinctions matter enormously in litigation because they directly influence reversibility. Two patients may experience the same septic deterioration and the same treatment delay, yet possess entirely different probabilities of recovery. One patient may retain sufficient reserve to survive aggressive intervention despite delayed escalation. Another may continue deteriorating despite appropriate treatment because meaningful physiologic compensation had already been exhausted.

Without Baseline Profiling, these differences may be overlooked entirely.

An attorney may initially focus on the visible delay while underestimating the degree of pre-existing decline already present within the patient's condition. Experts may later discover repeated admissions, progressive frailty, worsening organ dysfunction, and limited reserve that substantially alter the stability of the causation analysis.

The same delay does not carry the same physiologic meaning in every patient.

And in medical litigation, possibility must exist before causation can be sustained.

Clinical Intelligence Insight

Attorneys often focus on the visible event: the delayed transfer, the missed escalation, the worsening vital signs, or the catastrophic injury that followed.

But many cases are ultimately determined much earlier - within the patient's baseline physiology long before the alleged deviation ever occurred.

An attorney may initially believe the matter appears highly compelling because the deterioration seems preventable on preliminary review. Yet months later, after expert analysis and deeper physiologic profiling, the litigation strategy may begin shifting once the patient's limited reserve and poor reversibility become more apparent.

This is why Baseline Profiling cannot be treated as simple background medical history.

It determines whether the patient realistically possessed sufficient reserve for earlier intervention to meaningfully alter the clinical trajectory.

And in medical litigation, causation weakens rapidly once reversibility becomes physiologically unsustainable.

The Attorney Mistake

One of the most common mistakes in medical litigation is assuming that catastrophic outcome automatically establishes strong causation.
It does not.

Attorneys are naturally drawn toward cases involving death, paralysis, amputation, severe neurologic injury, or profound functional loss because the emotional gravity of those outcomes immediately creates the appearance of significant litigation exposure. Families often reinforce this perception. They describe the patient as "doing fine" before the event, insist the deterioration should have been recognized sooner, and believe earlier intervention would have changed everything.

At first review, the case may appear highly compelling.

The records may demonstrate delayed escalation, visible deterioration, or treatment intervals that initially seem concerning. Early expert review may even suggest the matter appears supportable from a causation standpoint.

But deeper Baseline Profiling often changes the entire analytical posture of the case.

Repeated admissions may reveal longstanding physiologic decline long before the final event occurred. Specialist documentation may demonstrate worsening cardiac function, progressive renal failure, chronic malnutrition, recurrent aspiration, advanced frailty, declining mobility, or steadily diminishing reserve over months or years preceding the alleged deviation.

The attorney who initially viewed the matter as a strong delay case may gradually discover that the patient's underlying condition had already severely limited reversibility before the critical event ever occurred.

This is where many cases begin shifting analytically.

The issue is no longer simply whether deterioration occurred or whether intervention should have happened earlier.

The more important question becomes whether earlier intervention probably would have altered the outcome in a meaningful and sustainable way.
That distinction fundamentally changes causation analysis.

Because medicine allows theoretical possibility in many situations. Litigation, however, requires something far more demanding than possibility alone.

It requires probability.

This is why Baseline Profiling cannot be treated as background medical history or secondary contextual information within the Lexcura Clinical Intelligence Model™.

It is one of the primary mechanisms through which causation stability is evaluated.

Without understanding the patient's reserve, frailty, recovery capacity, and overall baseline condition, even experienced attorneys may unintentionally overestimate the strength of causation simply because the outcome itself feels catastrophic.

And in medical litigation, catastrophic outcome alone does not establish reversibility.

Possibility Vs Probability

One of the most important distinctions in medical litigation is understanding the difference between medical possibility and legal probability.

Medicine frequently deals in possibility. Clinicians often acknowledge that earlier intervention, different treatment decisions, or more aggressive escalation may have altered a patient's course. In complex medicine, absolute certainty rarely exists, and multiple outcomes may remain theoretically conceivable even in critically ill patients.

Litigation, however, operates under a far more demanding standard.

The question is not whether earlier intervention could possibly have changed the outcome.

The question is whether the available evidence can establish that earlier intervention probably would have changed the outcome in a meaningful way.

This distinction becomes central during Baseline Profiling.

An elderly patient with advanced frailty, severe chronic illness, recurrent admissions, and progressive multi-organ decline may still possess theoretical survival possibility despite delayed intervention. But theoretical possibility alone does not establish sustainable causation.

Litigation requires more than retrospective possibility. It requires evidence capable of supporting probability.

This is where attorneys often encounter substantial difficulty in catastrophic cases.

Severe outcomes naturally create emotional pressure to believe the event must have been preventable. Families may strongly believe their loved one "would still be here" if treatment had occurred sooner. Even experts may initially feel drawn toward retrospective assumption when deterioration appears dramatic.

Yet as Baseline Profiling deepens, the analysis may begin shifting away from emotional causation and toward physiologic reality.

Advanced frailty, poor reserve, severe comorbid burden, chronic decline, and limited reversibility may substantially weaken the probability that earlier intervention would have meaningfully altered the outcome.

This does not necessarily mean the care was appropriate. Nor does it mean the delay lacked significance.

It means the evidence may be incapable of establishing that the alleged deviation probably changed the outcome with the level of certainty required to sustain causation under scrutiny.

This forms one of the central analytical principles of the Lexcura Clinical Intelligence Model™: Medicine allows possibility.

Litigation requires probability.

The Danger Of Retrospective Physiologic Assumption

One of the greatest analytical dangers in medical litigation is the tendency to evaluate a patient's condition retrospectively rather than physiologically.

After catastrophic outcome occurs, it becomes psychologically natural to assume that earlier intervention would have produced recovery. Death, paralysis, amputation, severe neurologic injury, or rapid deterioration often create the powerful impression that the patient was far more recoverable before the alleged deviation than the underlying physiology may actually support.

This is retrospective physiologic assumption.

The outcome itself begins influencing how the patient's prior condition is interpreted.

Attorneys, families, and even experts may unintentionally begin reconstructing the patient backward from the injury rather than evaluating the patient's actual reserve, chronic decline, comorbid burden, frailty, and recovery potential at the time intervention opportunity allegedly still existed.

This distinction becomes critically important during Baseline Profiling.

A patient who appears conversational, awake, or temporarily stable before deterioration may still possess profoundly limited reserve beneath the surface.

Recurrent hospitalizations, worsening organ dysfunction, progressive frailty, chronic malnutrition, declining mobility, escalating oxygen requirements, or steadily worsening cardiac and renal compromise may already indicate that reversibility was becoming increasingly limited long before the final event occurred.

Yet once catastrophic outcome occurs, hindsight often exaggerates the degree to which recovery seemed achievable beforehand.

This creates substantial causation risk within litigation analysis.

The question gradually shifts away from:
"What was the patient's actual physiologic condition before the alleged deviation occurred?"

And toward:
"How could this outcome have happened unless the event was preventable?"
Those are not the same question.

The first evaluates physiology objectively. The second evaluates outcome emotionally.

This is why Baseline Profiling must remain disciplined, evidence-based, and resistant to retrospective assumption.

Because in medical litigation, catastrophic outcome can easily create the illusion of reversibility even when the patient's underlying condition had already severely limited the probability of meaningful recovery long before the alleged delay ever occurred.

When Catastrophic Outcome Creates False Causation Pressure

Catastrophic outcomes create powerful retrospective pressure in medical litigation.

The more severe the injury, the more natural it becomes to assume that the outcome must have been preventable. Death, paralysis, amputation, profound neurologic injury, and permanent disability often create an immediate emotional belief that something significant must have gone wrong.

Families experience this pressure intensely because the deterioration feels sudden, devastating, and deeply personal. Attorneys may experience a similar reaction during early case review, particularly when the records appear to demonstrate visible delay, concerning vital signs, or escalating deterioration before intervention occurred.

In many cases, the initial litigation posture forms before Baseline Profiling has been fully completed.

This creates one of the greatest analytical dangers in medical litigation.

The severity of the outcome begins driving the causation analysis before the patient's actual physiologic reserve, reversibility, and recovery capacity have been evaluated carefully.

An attorney may initially view the matter as a highly compelling delay case. Experts may begin review believing earlier escalation should have occurred. Settlement discussions may even begin from the assumption that causation appears relatively strong.

But deeper analysis may later reveal a very different physiologic reality.

Repeated hospitalizations, chronic decline, worsening organ dysfunction, progressive frailty, advanced dementia, severe malnutrition, or limited reserve may demonstrate that the patient possessed extremely poor recovery potential long before the alleged deviation ever occurred. As this information emerges, the causation analysis often begins to shift.

The issue is no longer simply whether treatment should have occurred earlier.

The more important question becomes whether earlier intervention probably would have altered the outcome in a meaningful and sustainable way given the patient's underlying condition at the time.

This is where many emotionally compelling cases begin to weaken. Not because the outcome lacks significance.

Not because the family's suffering is unimportant.

And not necessarily because the care was appropriate.

The case weakens because catastrophic outcome alone does not establish physiologic reversibility.

This is one of the most important realities within Baseline Profiling.

The emotional severity of the outcome and the sustainability of causation are not always the same thing.

And in medical litigation, retrospective emotional pressure can never replace physiologic analysis.

Baseline Profiling And Settlement Strategy

Baseline Profiling does not only influence causation analysis. It often changes the entire strategic posture of litigation.

At intake, an attorney may view the matter as highly valuable because the injuries appear catastrophic and the alleged delay seems obvious on preliminary review.

Early chronology analysis may identify concerning escalation intervals, delayed intervention, or visible deterioration before transfer or treatment occurred.

Initially, the case may appear positioned for substantial settlement leverage.

But as deeper Baseline Profiling begins, the strategic landscape can change rapidly.

Repeated admissions may reveal longstanding physiologic decline. Specialist evaluations may document worsening prognosis months before the event in question.

Functional assessments may demonstrate progressive dependence, recurrent falls, malnutrition, severe frailty, or diminishing reserve long before the alleged deviation occurred.

As these findings emerge, expert confidence may begin shifting.

The issue is no longer simply whether earlier intervention should have occurred.

The more important question becomes whether earlier intervention probably would have altered the patient's long-term trajectory in a meaningful way.

This alters the causation framework and frequently changes litigation value.

A case that initially appeared highly compelling may become substantially more vulnerable once reversibility weakens under physiologic scrutiny. Settlement posture may shift accordingly. Experts who initially expressed confidence may become increasingly cautious as the patient's baseline condition is analyzed more closely.

Importantly, this process may occur even when the chronology itself remains relatively strong. The records may still support delayed escalation.

The deterioration may still be visible.

The intervention timing may still appear concerning.

Yet causation stability may continue weakening because Baseline Profiling demonstrates that the patient's recovery potential was already profoundly limited before the alleged deviation ever occurred.

It is one of the central mechanisms through which litigation strength, expert durability, and overall case value are evaluated within the Lexcura Clinical Intelligence Model™.

It is one of the central mechanisms through which litigation strength, causation sustainability, expert durability, and overall case value are evaluated.

Because in medical litigation, the severity of the outcome alone does not determine strategic strength.

The patient's underlying capacity for recovery often determines far more.

A case initially valued as catastrophic may become substantially more vulnerable once expert review determines that reserve and reversibility had already been severely limited before the alleged deviation occurred.

CASE ANALYSIS - 1

Strong Baseline Reserve Supporting Sustainable Causation

A 47-year-old female with no significant prior cardiac history presented to the emergency department with crushing chest pain, diaphoresis, nausea, and progressive shortness of breath. Prior records demonstrated that she remained fully independent, exercised regularly, maintained full-time employment, and possessed no meaningful functional impairment before the event in question.

Initial emergency department evaluation revealed evolving ischemic changes and elevated cardiac biomarkers consistent with acute myocardial infarction. Over the following several hours, the records demonstrated repeated episodes of worsening chest pain, progressive hemodynamic instability, and delayed transfer for definitive cardiac intervention despite visible deterioration.

The chronology itself remained relatively strong. Escalation timing could be reconstructed reliably, intervention opportunity could be identified clearly, and the records demonstrated a measurable delay between recognition of instability and definitive treatment.

Importantly, Baseline Profiling substantially strengthened the causation analysis.

The patient possessed strong reserve, meaningful recovery potential, and minimal pre-existing compromise before the event occurred. There was no evidence of advanced frailty, chronic organ failure, progressive functional decline, or severe baseline limitation that would independently weaken reversibility.

This baseline profile substantially strengthened the causation analysis.

Because the patient possessed substantial reserve before the delay occurred, earlier intervention carried a far greater probability of meaningfully altering the outcome.

Experts evaluating the matter were able to support causation with greater confidence because the patient's underlying condition remained capable of recovery at the time intervention opportunity still existed.

An attorney reviewing the case would not be forced to rely heavily upon retrospective assumption regarding reversibility. The patient's baseline condition itself supported the argument that reversibility remained realistically achievable before the deterioration progressed irreversibly.

As a result, Baseline Profiling strengthened the overall stability of the litigation analysis. Expert confidence remained stronger, causation became more sustainable, and the case maintained greater strategic leverage because the patient's baseline reserve supported the probability that earlier intervention could have altered the outcome meaningfully.

The strength of the case did not arise solely from the severity of the myocardial infarction. It arose from the combination of visible intervention opportunity, reliable chronology, and strong baseline reserve capable of supporting meaningful reversibility.

A defining principle of Baseline Profiling within the Lexcura Clinical Intelligence Model™: The same delay carries very different causation meaning depending upon the patient's underlying physiology.

CASE ANALYSIS - 2

Severe Baseline Compromise Weakening Causation Stability

An 89-year-old male with advanced congestive heart failure, severe chronic kidney disease, insulin-dependent diabetes, chronic obstructive pulmonary disease, recurrent aspiration pneumonia, and progressive dementia presented to a long term care facility with worsening respiratory distress, hypotension, confusion, and declining oxygen saturation.

Over the following several hours, the records demonstrated delayed physician notification, inconsistent reassessment intervals, and a late transfer to the emergency department. The patient was ultimately admitted with septic shock and multi-organ failure before dying several days later.

At intake, the matter appeared highly compelling.

The deterioration was visible. The delay in escalation appeared concerning. The family strongly believed earlier transfer would have prevented the patient's death, and preliminary review suggested possible failures in recognition and intervention timing.

The chronology itself remained relatively stable. The records allowed the escalation sequence, treatment delay, and progression of deterioration to be reconstructed with reasonable confidence.

But deeper Baseline Profiling gradually changed the direction of the analysis.

The patient's underlying condition revealed profound pre-existing compromise long before the alleged deviation occurred. Multiple admissions over the preceding year demonstrated steadily worsening cardiac function, progressive renal decline, recurrent pulmonary infections, chronic malnutrition, severe frailty, and substantial functional deterioration. Several specialists had already documented limited prognosis and poor long-term recovery potential prior to the final hospitalization.

As the patient's baseline condition became clearer, the causation analysis began to weaken.

The issue was no longer simply whether transfer should have occurred earlier.

The more important question became whether earlier intervention probably would have altered the outcome in a meaningful way given the patient's severely limited reserve at the time deterioration occurred.

This differentiation significantly changed the litigation posture of the case.

Experts who initially viewed the matter as a strong delay case became increasingly cautious as the patient's underlying physiology was analyzed more closely. Although earlier transfer may theoretically have altered portions of the clinical course, Baseline Profiling substantially weakened the probability that meaningful long-term recovery remained realistically achievable. Importantly, this did not necessarily mean the care was appropriate.

Nor did it eliminate the emotional significance of the patient's death.

But catastrophic outcome alone could not overcome the physiologic limitations already present long before the alleged deviation occurred.

As a result, the case gradually became more vulnerable from a causation standpoint despite the relatively stable chronology.

This is one of the most important principles within the Lexcura Clinical Intelligence Model™: Strong chronology alone does not establish strong causation.

The patient's baseline reserve ultimately determines whether meaningful reversibility was physiologically possible at all.

Applying Baseline Profiling Analysis

Understanding Baseline Profiling conceptually is only the beginning. The true importance of this pillar becomes apparent when the framework is applied within actual litigation analysis.

In practice, Baseline Profiling determines whether meaningful reversibility realistically existed before the alleged deviation occurred. It shapes how causation probability, intervention opportunity, expert confidence, and litigation strategy are ultimately evaluated.

The following exercise is designed to help apply these principles within a realistic litigation setting.

As you review the scenario, it is important to look beyond the visible deterioration and focus carefully on the patient's underlying condition before the event occurred.

Consider whether meaningful reserve still existed at the time intervention opportunity allegedly remained available. Evaluate whether the patient's baseline condition supports sustainable causation or whether the physiology itself substantially limits reversibility regardless of the delay being alleged.

This analytical breakpoint is the fulcrum of the analysis within the Lexcura Clinical Intelligence Model™.

Because chronology alone does not establish causation. Baseline physiology defines whether recovery potential was realistically possible in the first place.

Evaluating Baseline Reserve and Reversibility

A 79-year-old male with advanced congestive heart failure, chronic kidney disease, insulin-dependent diabetes, chronic obstructive pulmonary disease, and progressive frailty presented to the emergency department with worsening shortness of breath, fever, hypotension, and altered mental status.

The patient was admitted with suspected sepsis and respiratory compromise.

Over the following several hours, the records demonstrated delayed escalation, inconsistent reassessment intervals, and a measurable delay in ICU transfer despite progressive instability. Approximately twelve hours later, the patient developed respiratory failure requiring intubation and vasopressor support before later dying from multi-organ failure.

At intake, the case appeared highly concerning.

The family strongly believed earlier intervention would have prevented the patient's death. Preliminary review identified potentially delayed escalation and visible deterioration before ICU transfer occurred.

However, deeper Baseline Profiling revealed substantial pre-existing compromise.

Records from the preceding year demonstrated multiple admissions for worsening heart failure, recurrent pulmonary infections, declining renal function, progressive weight loss, impaired mobility, chronic malnutrition, and steadily worsening functional decline. Several specialists had already documented poor long-term prognosis and limited recovery potential prior to the final hospitalization.

As part of the Lexcura Clinical Intelligence Model™, your task is to evaluate whether the patient's baseline condition supports sustainable causation analysis.

Questions For Analysis

As you evaluate this case, consider not only whether deterioration and delayed escalation occurred, but whether the patient's underlying condition realistically supported meaningful reversibility at the time intervention opportunity allegedly remained available.

How does the patient's baseline condition influence the stability of the causation analysis? Consider the impact of advanced frailty, chronic organ dysfunction, recurrent admissions, declining functional status, and limited reserve on the probability that earlier intervention would have meaningfully altered the outcome.

To what extent does the chronology alone support sustainable causation in this matter? Does visible deterioration automatically establish that the patient possessed realistic recovery potential, or does Baseline Profiling substantially alter the interpretation of the delay itself? How might the patient's underlying physiology influence expert confidence during litigation? Consider whether the available evidence supports probability of reversibility or merely theoretical possibility.

As the case progresses, how might Baseline Profiling affect litigation strategy, settlement posture, and overall case value? Would deeper physiologic analysis likely strengthen the matter, weaken it, or create substantial vulnerability within the causation argument?

Most importantly, based upon the available information, does the evidence support the conclusion that earlier intervention probably would have altered the patient's long-term outcome in a meaningful and sustainable way? Or does the patient's baseline condition substantially limit the stability of that conclusion under scrutiny?

Answer Key & Analysis

The central analytical issue in this case is not simply whether delayed escalation occurred. The deeper issue is whether the patient possessed sufficient reserve for earlier intervention to have probably altered the outcome in a meaningful and sustainable way.

At first review, the matter appears highly concerning. The deterioration is visible, escalation delays appear potentially significant, and the patient ultimately suffers catastrophic outcome following progressive instability. An attorney evaluating the chronology alone may initially view the case as possessing strong causation potential.

However, deeper Baseline Profiling substantially changes the stability of the analysis.

The patient demonstrated advanced multi-system compromise long before the final hospitalization occurred. Recurrent admissions, progressive heart failure, worsening pulmonary disease, declining renal function, chronic malnutrition, impaired mobility, and steadily worsening frailty all suggest severely limited reserve prior to the alleged deviation itself.

This changes the analysis substantially because the patient's underlying physiology directly influences reversibility.

Although earlier escalation and ICU transfer may theoretically have altered portions of the clinical course, the available evidence may not support the probability that meaningful long-term recovery remained realistically achievable at the time deterioration occurred.

As a result, the causation analysis becomes substantially more vulnerable under scrutiny. This does not necessarily mean the care was appropriate.

Nor does it eliminate the significance of the delay itself.

But Baseline Profiling weakens the argument that earlier intervention probably would have changed the ultimate outcome in a sustainable way given the patient's severely compromised condition before the event occurred.

Importantly, the chronology alone cannot resolve this question.

The records may still support delayed escalation and visible deterioration. Yet chronology without reserve does not automatically establish meaningful reversibility.

This is one of the central analytical principles within the Lexcura Clinical Intelligence Model™: The probability that outcome could have been altered depends not only upon timing, but upon whether the patient's underlying condition still allowed recovery to remain realistically achievable at all.

And in medical litigation, possibility alone is rarely sufficient to sustain causation under scrutiny.

Chapter 2 Takeaways

Baseline Profiling

1. Baseline defines possibility before causation can be evaluated responsibly.

Before litigation can determine whether a delay altered outcome, the patient's underlying reserve, frailty, recovery capacity, and overall condition must first be understood.

2. *Chronology alone does not establish causation.*

A visible delay, worsening deterioration, or concerning escalation interval does not automatically prove that meaningful survival potential remained realistically achievable at the time intervention opportunity still existed.

3. *Severe outcome does not automatically establish reversibility.*

Catastrophic injury naturally creates emotional pressure to assume preventability. However, severe outcome alone cannot establish that the patient possessed sufficient reserve for earlier intervention to probably alter the trajectory meaningfully.

4. *The same delay may carry profoundly different causation significance depending upon the patient's baseline reserve.*

A previously healthy patient with strong reserve may possess substantial recovery potential despite delayed intervention. A severely frail patient with advanced chronic decline may possess limited reversibility long before the alleged deviation occurs.

5. *Medicine allows possibility. Litigation requires probability.*

Theoretical survival possibility is not the same as sustainable causation. Litigation requires evidence capable of supporting the probability that earlier intervention would have meaningfully altered the outcome.

6. *Frailty significantly alters litigation analysis.*

Progressive functional decline, chronic illness, recurrent admissions, malnutrition, organ dysfunction, and diminished reserve may substantially weaken reversibility even when deterioration and delay remain visible within the records.

7. Baseline Profiling directly influences expert confidence and litigation strategy.

As deeper profiling reveals worsening reserve and limited recovery capacity, experts may become increasingly cautious regarding sustainable causation, which may significantly alter settlement posture and overall case value.

8. Emotional causation pressure cannot replace physiologic analysis.

Families, attorneys, and even experts may initially assume that catastrophic deterioration must have been preventable. Baseline Profiling helps distinguish emotionally compelling outcomes from physiologically sustainable causation.

9. Reversibility is one of the central questions in medical litigation.

The issue is not simply whether deterioration occurred. The issue is whether the patient still possessed clinically significant recovery potential at the time intervention opportunity allegedly remained available.

10. Possibility must exist before causation can be sustained.

This is one of the foundational principles of the Lexcura Clinical Intelligence Model™. Before timing can alter outcome, the patient's underlying condition must first allow meaningful recovery potential to remain realistically achievable at all.

Transition To The Next Pillar

Once Baseline Profiling establishes whether meaningful recovery was physiologically possible, the next question becomes equally important:

When did deterioration become identifiable, and when did intervention opportunity begin narrowing?

A patient may possess substantial reserve and meaningful recovery potential, yet causation analysis can still weaken if the chronology cannot establish when instability became visible, when escalation thresholds were reached, or when intervention opportunity realistically remained available.

This is where Timeline Reconstruction becomes critical.
Because in medical litigation, timing is not simply a sequence of events. Timing defines recognition, escalation opportunity, intervention delay, and the narrowing window in which outcome may still have remained alterable.

Two cases may involve the same diagnosis and the same ultimate injury, yet possess entirely different litigation trajectories depending upon how clearly deterioration progression can be reconstructed over time.

The next pillar examines how clinical events are organized into defensible chronology, how escalation windows are identified, how intervention opportunity is evaluated, and how temporal reconstruction ultimately shapes causation stability itself. Because before litigation can determine whether timing altered outcome, the progression of deterioration must first be reconstructed clearly enough to identify when meaningful opportunity still existed.

Because in medical litigation, timing alone cannot overcome physiology already approaching irreversible decline.

CHAPTER - 03

TIMELINE RECONSTRUCTION

Reconstructing the sequence of clinical deterioration.

This chapter establishes a foundational pillar within the Lexcura Clinical Intelligence Model™ creating the evidentiary framework required for defensible medical-legal analysis.

DEFINING ESCALATION OPPORTUNITY BEFORE OUTCOME

At intake, the chronology appeared devastating.

A 52-year-old male presented to the emergency department with fever, tachycardia, hypotension, worsening abdominal pain, and progressive confusion following several days of persistent gastrointestinal symptoms. Initial nursing documentation identified concerning vital sign abnormalities, elevated lactate, and increasing instability shortly after arrival.

Over the following several hours, the patient's condition continued deteriorating.

Repeated assessments demonstrated worsening hypotension, declining urine output, increasing tachypnea, escalating oxygen requirements, and progressive mental status changes. Nursing documentation reflected growing concern regarding possible sepsis and worsening hemodynamic compromise. Multiple reassessments documented persistent instability before physician escalation and ICU consultation ultimately occurred.

By the time definitive intervention was initiated, the patient had already developed septic shock with multi-organ failure requiring vasopressor support, mechanical ventilation, and emergency surgical intervention. He later suffered permanent renal impairment and severe functional decline following prolonged hospitalization.

The family believed the deterioration should have been recognized much earlier. The attorney initially agreed.

At first review, the timeline appeared to demonstrate multiple missed opportunities for escalation and delayed recognition of progressive instability. The records suggested that deterioration had been visible long before definitive intervention occurred.

But as the analysis progressed, the chronology became far more complex. The central issue was no longer simply whether deterioration occurred.

The more important question became when the deterioration became sufficiently identifiable to create a reasonable escalation obligation and whether meaningful intervention opportunity still existed during each stage of progression.

That distinction forms the foundation of Timeline Reconstruction within the Lexcura Clinical Intelligence Model™.

Because in medical litigation, deterioration is rarely instantaneous.

Clinical instability usually evolves progressively over time through changing vital signs, worsening assessments, evolving laboratory abnormalities, escalating symptoms, declining physiologic compensation, and narrowing intervention opportunity.

Timeline Reconstruction is the process through which those events are organized into defensible clinical sequence.

It asks when deterioration first became identifiable, when escalation reasonably should have occurred, when intervention opportunity began narrowing, and at what point delay began carrying meaningful causation significance.

These questions fundamentally shape litigation analysis. Because timing in medical litigation is not merely chronological. Timing defines opportunity.

And before causation can be evaluated responsibly, the progression of deterioration must first be reconstructed clearly enough to determine when meaningful intervention opportunity still existed.

Transition To The Next Pillar

Within the Lexcura Clinical Intelligence Model™, Timeline Reconstruction refers to the structured analysis of clinical progression over time. It examines how deterioration evolved, when instability became identifiable, how escalation opportunities emerged, and whether intervention windows remained realistically available as the patient's condition changed.

The purpose of Timeline Reconstruction is not simply to place events into chronological order.

It is to determine how clinical reality unfolded moment by moment within the context of recognition, reassessment, escalation, intervention opportunity, and progressive physiologic decline.

This distinction becomes critically important in medical litigation because chronology alone does not automatically establish meaningful delay.

A timestamp by itself rarely determines causation.

The analytical question is whether the patient's deterioration had progressed sufficiently at a given point in time to create a reasonable obligation for reassessment, escalation, intervention, or higher-level response.

This is why Timeline Reconstruction functions as far more than organizational sequencing.

Two patients may ultimately experience the same catastrophic outcome while possessing entirely different litigation timelines.

In one case, deterioration may progress gradually with subtle warning signs and evolving instability over many hours before escalation obligations become reasonably identifiable. In another, severe deterioration may become visible rapidly with clear escalation thresholds emerging much earlier in the progression.

The chronology itself may appear similar on superficial review. The clinical meaning of the timeline may be profoundly different.

This is why Timeline Reconstruction serves as one of the central analytical pillars of the Lexcura Clinical Intelligence Model™.

Because before litigation can determine whether delay altered outcome, the progression of deterioration must first be reconstructed clearly enough to identify when meaningful intervention opportunity actually existed.

The Difference Between Clock Time And Clinical Time

One of the most important concepts in medical litigation is understanding that clock time and clinical time are not always the same thing.

Two hours on a clock may appear identical within the records. Physiologically, however, those same two hours may carry profoundly different significance depending upon the patient's condition during the progression of deterioration.

A stable postoperative patient with mild discomfort may tolerate several hours without meaningful change in outcome trajectory. A septic patient experiencing worsening hypotension, escalating lactate, declining oxygenation, and progressive organ dysfunction may lose meaningful intervention opportunity minute by minute during the same period of time.

This distinction fundamentally changes Timeline Reconstruction.

Medical litigation often focuses heavily on timestamps such as when the provider was notified, when the physician responded, when reassessment occurred, when transfer was initiated, or when intervention ultimately took place.

Those timestamps matter.

But timestamps alone do not define causation significance.

The more important issue is what was happening physiologically during the interval itself.

A seemingly brief delay may carry enormous clinical significance if the patient was deteriorating rapidly during that period. Conversely, a longer interval may carry far less causation weight if the patient's condition remained relatively stable without meaningful progression of instability.

This is why Timeline Reconstruction cannot focus solely on elapsed time.

It must evaluate the relationship between progression, recognition, escalation, physiologic decline, and narrowing intervention opportunity.

Attorneys often encounter difficulty here because retrospective review naturally compresses the timeline after catastrophic outcome occurs. Once the injury is known, deterioration may appear "obvious" in hindsight even when the progression was evolving more gradually in real time.

Timeline Reconstruction helps separate retrospective certainty from real-time clinical visibility.

Because in medical litigation, the significance of time is not determined solely by minutes passing on a clock.

It is determined by what was happening to the patient while those minutes were passing.

When Deterioration Becomes Identifiable

One of the most contested questions in medical litigation is determining when deterioration became sufficiently identifiable to create a reasonable obligation for escalation or intervention.

This question is rarely as simple as it appears in hindsight.

Catastrophic deterioration often feels sudden once the final outcome is known. Yet clinical instability typically evolves progressively through changing assessments, worsening vital signs, abnormal laboratory trends, increasing oxygen requirements, altered mental status, declining urine output, escalating pain, or subtle shifts in overall presentation before full decompensation ultimately occurs.

Timeline Reconstruction examines how those warning signs emerged over time. The analytical issue is not simply whether abnormal findings existed.

The issue is when the pattern of deterioration became sufficiently recognizable that a reasonable clinician should have identified escalating risk within the context of the patient's overall condition.

This differentiation becomes materially significant to the analysis. A mildly abnormal heart rate in isolation may carry little significance. The same heart rate occurring alongside hypotension, worsening respiratory distress, altered mental status, declining oxygen saturation, rising lactate, and repeated reassessment concerns may carry profoundly different clinical meaning.

Deterioration often becomes identifiable cumulatively rather than instantaneously.

This is why Timeline Reconstruction focuses heavily on trend recognition rather than isolated findings alone.

A patient's condition may appear relatively manageable at one point in the progression, then evolve into a clearly unstable pattern as additional abnormalities emerge over time. Determining when that transition occurred is often central to litigation analysis.

Attorneys frequently encounter difficulty here because retrospective review naturally makes progressive deterioration appear more obvious after catastrophic outcome occurs. Once the final injury is known, earlier warning signs may seem unmistakable even when they were evolving more gradually in real time.

Timeline Reconstruction helps distinguish between subtle early instability and clinically actionable deterioration.

Because in medical litigation, escalation obligations are not determined solely by isolated abnormalities.

They are determined by when the overall progression of deterioration became sufficiently identifiable to create meaningful intervention opportunity.

Escalation Opportunity Vs Hindsight

One of the most important principles in Timeline Reconstruction is understanding that providers must be evaluated based upon what was reasonably identifiable at the time decisions were being made - not solely through the clarity created by retrospective outcome.

This distinction is critically important in medical litigation because hindsight naturally alters how deterioration is perceived.

Once catastrophic injury occurs, earlier abnormalities often appear far more obvious than they may have seemed during the actual progression of care. Warning signs that later appear unmistakable may initially have emerged gradually, inconsistently, or within a broader clinical picture containing competing explanations, overlapping comorbidities, or fluctuating presentation.

Timeline Reconstruction helps separate retrospective certainty from real-time clinical visibility.

A patient experiencing early sepsis, evolving hemorrhage, neurologic decline, or progressive respiratory compromise may not initially present with dramatic instability. Deterioration often develops incrementally through subtle physiologic changes that become increasingly recognizable only as the progression continues.

This is where escalation opportunity becomes central to litigation analysis. The issue is not simply whether the patient ultimately deteriorated.

The issue is when the progression became sufficiently identifiable that a reasonable clinician should have recognized increasing risk and responded accordingly within the context of the information available at that specific point in time.

This distinction fundamentally shapes Standard of Care analysis later in the model.

Because providers are not expected to predict future outcome with perfect hindsight. They are expected to respond reasonably to the clinical information that was visible and reasonably identifiable during the actual progression itself.

Attorneys frequently encounter difficulty here because retrospective review compresses uncertainty. Once the final injury is known, the earlier progression may appear linear and obvious even when the real-time presentation was evolving more ambiguously.

Timeline Reconstruction restores temporal context to the analysis.

It examines what was visible, when it became visible, how the progression evolved, and whether meaningful escalation opportunity realistically existed before irreversible deterioration occurred.

Because in medical litigation, hindsight may clarify outcome.

But liability depends upon what was reasonably identifiable before the outcome was known.

Clinical Intelligence Warning

One of the most dangerous misconceptions in medical litigation is assuming that a patient who appears temporarily stable is physiologically stable.

They are not always the same thing.

A patient may still be awake, conversational, interactive, or hemodynamically compensated while significant deterioration is already progressing beneath the surface. Early sepsis, internal hemorrhage, neurologic compromise, respiratory decline, and evolving shock frequently develop progressively before catastrophic instability becomes externally obvious.

This creates substantial analytical risk during retrospective review.

Once catastrophic outcome occurs, attorneys, families, and even experts may look backward through the records and assume the deterioration should have been unmistakable much earlier in the progression. Yet real-time clinical deterioration often evolves through subtle trend changes rather than immediate collapse.

A patient's blood pressure may still appear technically acceptable while compensatory tachycardia worsens. Oxygen saturation may remain temporarily preserved despite increasing respiratory effort. Mental status changes may emerge gradually rather than dramatically.

Laboratory abnormalities may evolve progressively before irreversible physiologic decline becomes fully apparent.

Timeline Reconstruction helps distinguish between apparent stability and true physiologic stability.

Because compensation is not the same as recovery.

And in medical litigation, a patient may appear clinically stable long before the underlying physiology begins approaching irreversible deterioration.

The Attorney Mistake

One of the most common mistakes in medical litigation is focusing too heavily on the final catastrophic event while underestimating the progression that occurred beforehand.

Attorneys are naturally drawn toward the moment everything visibly collapsed - the cardiac arrest, respiratory failure, emergency intubation, ICU transfer, or irreversible neurologic injury.

Those moments feel decisive because they are dramatic, emotionally powerful, and easy to identify within the records.

But Timeline Reconstruction rarely begins at the point of collapse. It begins much earlier.

In many cases, the most important escalation opportunities emerge during the progressive deterioration leading up to the catastrophic event itself. Subtle instability, worsening reassessment findings, abnormal trend progression, escalating oxygen requirements, increasing confusion, declining urine output, or evolving laboratory abnormalities may all begin narrowing intervention opportunity long before full decompensation occurs.

This distinction becomes important during litigation analysis.

An attorney may initially focus on the final injury while overlooking the earlier progression that actually defines the causation timeline. Yet the litigation significance of the case often depends less on the moment of collapse and more on whether the deterioration should reasonably have been recognized and escalated earlier in the sequence.

Timeline Reconstruction shifts the analysis away from isolated catastrophic outcome and back toward progressive clinical evolution.

Because in medical litigation, causation rarely develops from one isolated moment alone.

It usually develops through a sequence of narrowing intervention opportunities occurring before the final injury becomes irreversible.

The Danger Of Retrospective Timeline Compression

One of the greatest analytical dangers in medical litigation is retrospective timeline compression.

After catastrophic outcome occurs, the entire progression of deterioration often appears far more rapid, obvious, and linear than it actually appeared in real time.

Events that unfolded gradually over many hours may later feel compressed into a sequence that seems unmistakably emergent in hindsight.

This distortion occurs naturally.

Once attorneys, families, experts, and juries know the final outcome, earlier warning signs begin carrying far greater significance retrospectively than they may have carried during the actual progression itself.

Subtle instability that initially evolved incrementally may later appear glaringly obvious once the patient ultimately suffers cardiac arrest, respiratory collapse, stroke, septic shock, or irreversible neurologic injury.

Timeline Reconstruction helps correct this distortion by restoring temporal context to the analysis.

A patient's deterioration may initially have appeared intermittent, partially responsive to intervention, complicated by chronic illness, or evolving within a broader clinical picture containing competing diagnostic possibilities. Warning signs that later appear unmistakable may not initially have crossed clear escalation thresholds during the earlier stages of progression.

This distinction is critically important.

Because litigation often evaluates a progression retrospectively while clinicians were forced to evaluate it prospectively in real time without knowledge of the final outcome.

That difference fundamentally alters how escalation opportunity must be analyzed.

Timeline Reconstruction examines how the progression actually unfolded moment by moment rather than allowing hindsight to artificially compress the sequence into an apparently obvious pathway toward catastrophe.

Because in medical litigation, the clarity created by outcome can easily distort the uncertainty that existed before the outcome was known.

Timeline Reconstruction And Settlement Strategy

Timeline Reconstruction does not only influence causation analysis. It often shapes the entire strategic direction of litigation.

At intake, an attorney may initially view the matter as highly compelling because the records appear to demonstrate visible deterioration before catastrophic outcome occurred. Preliminary review may identify delayed escalation, concerning reassessment gaps, prolonged transfer intervals, or progressive instability preceding irreversible injury.

Initially, the chronology may appear highly favorable from a causation standpoint. But as Timeline Reconstruction deepens, the stability of the sequence itself often becomes central to litigation strategy.

A well-constructed timeline may substantially strengthen the case by clearly establishing progressive deterioration, visible escalation opportunity, delayed response, and narrowing intervention windows over time. Expert opinions become more durable when the chronology can demonstrate precisely when instability became identifiable and how the progression evolved before irreversible decline occurred.

Conversely, unstable timelines frequently weaken litigation sustainability even when the outcome itself remains catastrophic.

Conflicting timestamps, inconsistent reassessment intervals, unclear escalation visibility, incomplete nursing documentation, delayed charting, fragmented communication records, or uncertainty regarding when deterioration became clinically actionable may all destabilize the chronology substantially.

This distinction often changes settlement posture.

A case that initially appeared highly valuable may become increasingly vulnerable once expert review determines that escalation opportunity cannot be reconstructed with sufficient clarity to support sustainable causation under scrutiny.

Importantly, this process may occur even when the patient ultimately suffered devastating injury.

The severity of the outcome alone cannot stabilize an unclear timeline.

Because in medical litigation, causation depends not only upon what happened, but upon whether the progression of deterioration can be reconstructed clearly enough to establish when meaningful intervention opportunity actually existed.

This is why Timeline Reconstruction functions as one of the central strategic pillars within the Lexcura Clinical Intelligence Model™.

It determines whether the chronology can sustain defensible escalation analysis, durable expert opinion, and reliable causation sequencing before litigation strategy fully develops.

CASE ANALYSIS - 1

Stable Timeline Supporting Sustainable Escalation Analysis

A 61-year-old female presented to the emergency department with fever, tachycardia, hypotension, worsening shortness of breath, and increasing confusion following several days of progressive respiratory symptoms. Initial nursing assessments documented abnormal vital signs, elevated respiratory rate, declining oxygen saturation, and visible signs of worsening instability shortly after arrival.

Over the following several hours, the records demonstrated progressive deterioration with unusual clarity.

Repeated reassessments documented worsening hypotension, increasing oxygen requirements, declining mental status, rising lactate levels, and persistent tachycardia despite fluid administration and supportive treatment. Nursing documentation reflected escalating concern regarding possible sepsis progression and worsening respiratory compromise. Physician notification times, reassessment intervals, laboratory progression, and escalation discussions remained consistently documented throughout the sequence.

Most importantly, the chronology allowed the progression of deterioration to be reconstructed reliably.

The records established when instability first became identifiable, when escalation thresholds became clinically significant, when providers were notified, and how intervention opportunity progressively narrowed over time.

As Timeline Reconstruction deepened, the causation analysis became substantially stronger. The patient's deterioration did not appear sudden or unforeseeable in retrospect.

The progression demonstrated a visible pattern of worsening instability occurring over multiple hours before definitive escalation and ICU transfer ultimately occurred.

Expert reviewers were able to identify a relatively clear interval during which earlier intervention may reasonably have altered the trajectory before irreversible physiologic decline developed fully.

This distinction became critically important.

Because the chronology remained stable, the litigation analysis did not depend heavily upon retrospective assumption or speculative reconstruction. The escalation sequence could be defended through documented progression rather than inferred through hindsight alone.

An attorney reviewing the case would be able to demonstrate progressive deterioration, visible escalation opportunity, delayed intervention, and narrowing treatment windows through a chronology capable of withstanding scrutiny.

As a result, Timeline Reconstruction substantially strengthened causation sustainability, expert durability, and overall litigation stability.

The strength of the case did not arise solely from the severity of the patient's septic shock.

It arose from the ability to reconstruct the progression of deterioration clearly enough to identify when meaningful escalation opportunity still existed before irreversible decline occurred.

This is one of the central principles of Timeline Reconstruction within the Lexcura Clinical Intelligence Model™: Strong causation often depends less on the final catastrophic event and more on the ability to reconstruct the progression leading to it.

CASE ANALYSIS - 2

Unstable Timeline Weakening Escalation Analysis

A 73-year-old male with chronic obstructive pulmonary disease, diabetes, chronic kidney disease, and moderate baseline frailty presented to the emergency department with worsening weakness, fever, confusion, and shortness of breath.

Initial assessments documented mild hypotension, tachycardia, elevated respiratory rate, and intermittent oxygen desaturation.

Several hours later, the patient suffered respiratory failure requiring intubation before later developing septic shock and multi-organ dysfunction.

At intake, the chronology initially appeared highly concerning.

The family believed the deterioration had been obvious for hours before escalation occurred. Preliminary review suggested delayed physician notification, inconsistent reassessment intervals, and possible failures in recognizing worsening instability before respiratory collapse developed.

But as Timeline Reconstruction progressed, the chronology itself became increasingly unstable.

Nursing documentation contained inconsistent reassessment timing during critical portions of the progression. Several vital sign entries appeared delayed or retrospectively charted.

Communication records between nursing staff and providers were fragmented, and portions of the escalation sequence could not be reconstructed clearly from the available documentation.

Most importantly, the precise point at which deterioration became clinically actionable grew increasingly difficult to define.

The patient demonstrated periods of partial stabilization intermixed with worsening abnormalities. Oxygen saturation fluctuated. Blood pressure temporarily improved following intervention before later declining again. Mental status changes appeared intermittently throughout the progression rather than through one clearly identifiable escalation point.

As a result, the chronology became substantially more vulnerable to interpretive disagreement.

Experts reviewing the matter could not identify a single clearly defensible moment at which escalation obligation became unquestionably obvious. Instead, the progression evolved through a series of gradually worsening abnormalities whose significance became far clearer retrospectively after catastrophic deterioration ultimately occurred.

This distinction significantly weakened the stability of the causation analysis. The issue was no longer simply whether deterioration occurred.

The more important question became whether Timeline Reconstruction could establish with sufficient clarity when meaningful escalation opportunity realistically existed before irreversible decline developed.

Importantly, this did not necessarily mean the care was appropriate.

Nor did it eliminate the seriousness of the patient's outcome.

But unstable chronology substantially weakened the ability to support durable escalation analysis without increasing reliance upon retrospective interpretation and hindsight reconstruction.

As a result, expert confidence became more cautious, causation sequencing became less stable, and the litigation posture gradually became more vulnerable despite the severity of the final injury.

This is one of the most important principles within the Lexcura Clinical Intelligence Model™:

Catastrophic outcome alone does not stabilize an unclear timeline.

Strong causation depends upon the ability to reconstruct when deterioration became sufficiently identifiable to create meaningful escalation opportunity before irreversible decline occurred.

Applying Timeline Reconstruction Analysis

Understanding Timeline Reconstruction conceptually is only the beginning. The true importance of this pillar becomes apparent when the framework is applied within actual litigation analysis.

In practice, Timeline Reconstruction determines whether deterioration progression can be reconstructed clearly enough to establish when instability became identifiable, when escalation obligations reasonably emerged, and whether meaningful intervention opportunity still existed before irreversible decline occurred.

The following exercise is designed to apply these principles within a realistic litigation setting.

As you review the scenario, it is important to look beyond the final catastrophic event and focus carefully on how the progression evolved over time. Consider when deterioration first became clinically recognizable, whether escalation opportunity narrowed progressively, and whether the chronology can establish a defensible sequence of recognition, reassessment, escalation, and intervention opportunity.

This distinction is central within the Lexcura Clinical Intelligence Model™. Because catastrophic outcome alone does not establish delayed escalation.

Timeline Reconstruction must first determine whether the progression of deterioration can identify when meaningful intervention opportunity realistically existed before irreversible decline developed.

Evaluating Escalation Opportunity and Temporal Progression

A 64-year-old female presented to the emergency department with fever, productive cough, worsening weakness, tachycardia, and increasing shortness of breath following several days of progressive respiratory illness.

Initial nursing documentation reflected mild hypotension, elevated respiratory rate, intermittent oxygen desaturation, and increasing fatigue. Laboratory evaluation demonstrated elevated white blood cell count and rising lactate levels. The patient received intravenous fluids, antibiotics, and supplemental oxygen while awaiting further physician reassessment.

Over the following several hours, the records demonstrated worsening oxygen requirements, progressive tachypnea, intermittent hypotension, increasing confusion, declining urine output, and repeated nursing reassessment concerns regarding possible sepsis progression.

Approximately eight hours after arrival, the patient suffered acute respiratory failure requiring emergency intubation and ICU transfer before later developing septic shock and multi-organ dysfunction.

At intake, the case appeared highly concerning.

The family strongly believed the deterioration had been obvious long before respiratory collapse occurred. Preliminary review suggested delayed escalation, prolonged reassessment intervals, and possible failure to recognize progressive instability before irreversible decline developed.

However, deeper Timeline Reconstruction revealed a more complex progression.

Vital signs fluctuated throughout the sequence. Some abnormalities improved temporarily following treatment before worsening again. Mental status changes appeared intermittently. Several reassessment intervals remained relatively stable before rapid deterioration later accelerated over a shorter period of time.

As part of the Lexcura Clinical Intelligence Model™, your task is to evaluate whether the chronology can establish a stable and defensible escalation sequence capable of supporting sustainable causation analysis.

Questions For Analysis

As you evaluate this case, consider not only whether deterioration ultimately occurred, but whether the chronology can establish when the progression became sufficiently identifiable to create a reasonable escalation obligation.

At what point did the patient's deterioration become clinically actionable within the context of the overall progression? Consider how the evolving vital signs, worsening oxygen requirements, mental status changes, laboratory abnormalities, and reassessment findings influenced escalation visibility over time.

How does the fluctuating nature of the patient's condition affect Timeline

Reconstruction? Do temporary periods of stabilization weaken the clarity of escalation opportunity, or does the overall progression still demonstrate a recognizable pattern of worsening instability?

To what extent does the chronology support sustainable causation analysis? Can the records establish a defensible interval during which earlier intervention probably would have altered the trajectory before irreversible decline developed?

How might retrospective review influence interpretation of the progression? Consider whether the deterioration appears more obvious after the catastrophic outcome than it may have appeared during the actual sequence of care.

As the case progresses, how might Timeline Reconstruction influence expert confidence, litigation strategy, and settlement posture? Would the chronology likely strengthen the causation analysis, weaken it, or create substantial disagreement regarding when escalation obligations reasonably emerged?

Most importantly, based upon the available sequence, can the timeline establish with sufficient clarity when meaningful intervention opportunity still existed before respiratory failure and irreversible physiologic decline occurred?

Answer Key & Analysis

The central analytical issue in this case is not simply whether respiratory failure ultimately occurred. The deeper issue is whether the chronology can establish when deterioration became sufficiently identifiable to create a reasonable escalation obligation before irreversible decline developed.

At first review, the matter appears highly concerning.

The patient demonstrated worsening oxygen requirements, progressive tachypnea, intermittent hypotension, increasing confusion, rising lactate levels, and repeated reassessment concerns before ultimately suffering respiratory failure and septic shock. An attorney reviewing the sequence initially may view the chronology as strongly supportive of delayed escalation and preventable deterioration.

However, deeper Timeline Reconstruction reveals a more complex progression.

The deterioration did not evolve through one continuous, unmistakable decline.

Instead, the patient experienced fluctuating instability throughout portions of the sequence. Certain abnormalities temporarily improved following intervention before worsening again. Some reassessment periods appeared relatively stable before rapid acceleration of deterioration later developed.

This distinction substantially alters the analysis.

Because Timeline Reconstruction does not evaluate deterioration retrospectively from the final outcome alone. It evaluates how recognizable the progression actually appeared during the real-time sequence itself.

Although the records demonstrate worsening instability overall, the chronology may not establish one clearly identifiable moment at which escalation obligation became unquestionably obvious. Instead, the progression evolved through accumulating abnormalities whose collective significance became increasingly apparent over time.

As a result, expert interpretation may begin diverging regarding when meaningful intervention opportunity realistically existed.

Some experts may conclude that the overall pattern of worsening instability should have prompted earlier ICU escalation or more aggressive intervention before respiratory collapse occurred. Others may argue that the fluctuating progression, intermittent stabilization, and evolving presentation made the escalation threshold less definitive during earlier portions of the timeline.

This distinction substantially changes the analysis during causation analysis. The issue is no longer simply whether deterioration occurred.

The issue is whether Timeline Reconstruction can establish with sufficient clarity when the progression became actionable enough that earlier intervention probably would have altered the trajectory before irreversible physiologic decline developed.

Importantly, this does not necessarily eliminate potential liability.

Nor does it diminish the seriousness of the patient's outcome.

But fluctuating chronology may substantially weaken the stability of escalation analysis by increasing reliance upon retrospective interpretation rather than clearly identifiable real-time progression.

This is one of the central principles of Timeline Reconstruction within the Lexcura Clinical Intelligence Model™: Strong causation depends not only upon catastrophic outcome, but upon the ability to reconstruct when deterioration became sufficiently recognizable to create meaningful intervention opportunity before irreversible decline occurred.

Chapter 3 Takeaways

Timeline Reconstruction

1. *Timeline defines opportunity before causation can be evaluated responsibly.*

Before litigation can determine whether delay altered outcome, the progression of deterioration must first be reconstructed clearly enough to identify when meaningful intervention opportunity still existed.

2. *Chronology alone does not establish delayed escalation.*

A sequence of timestamps does not automatically determine liability. The critical issue is when deterioration became sufficiently identifiable to create a reasonable escalation obligation within the context of the patient's overall progression.

3. *Clock time and clinical time are not always the same.*

Two hours on a clock may carry profoundly different causation significance depending upon what was happening physiologically during the progression itself.

4. *Deterioration is often progressive before it becomes catastrophic.*

Clinical instability frequently develops through evolving assessments, worsening trends, escalating oxygen requirements, abnormal laboratory progression, and narrowing physiologic compensation long before irreversible collapse ultimately occurs.

5. *Escalation obligations emerge through recognizable progression.*

Isolated abnormalities may not independently establish clear escalation responsibility. Timeline Reconstruction evaluates when the overall pattern of deterioration became clinically actionable within the context of the evolving sequence.

6. *Retrospective review often compresses the timeline artificially.*

Once catastrophic outcome occurs, earlier warning signs frequently appear more obvious in hindsight than they may have appeared during the actual progression of care.

7. *Apparent stability does not always equal physiologic stability.*

A patient may remain awake, conversational, or temporarily compensated while meaningful deterioration continues progressing beneath the surface.

8. *Strong timelines strengthen expert durability and litigation stability.*

When deterioration progression, escalation opportunity, and intervention timing can be reconstructed clearly, expert opinions become more sustainable and causation analysis becomes more defensible under scrutiny.

9. *Unstable chronology weakens causation sequencing.*

Conflicting documentation, fluctuating progression, inconsistent reassessment intervals, and unclear escalation thresholds may substantially weaken the ability to establish when meaningful intervention opportunity actually existed.

10. Catastrophic outcome alone does not stabilize an unclear timeline.

This is one of the foundational principles of the Lexcura Clinical Intelligence Model™. Strong causation depends not only upon the final injury, but upon the ability to reconstruct when deterioration became sufficiently identifiable to create meaningful escalation opportunity before irreversible decline occurred.

Transition To The Next Pillar

Once Timeline Reconstruction establishes when deterioration became identifiable and when intervention opportunity began narrowing, the next question becomes equally important:

Given what was knowable at the time, what clinical obligations reasonably existed?

A patient may possess meaningful recovery potential. The chronology may clearly demonstrate progressive deterioration and visible escalation opportunity. Yet litigation analysis still cannot determine liability until the actual standard of care is evaluated within the context of the information reasonably available during the progression itself.

This is where Standard of Care Review becomes critical.

Because in medical litigation, poor outcome alone does not establish breach.

Providers are not evaluated based upon perfect hindsight or idealized outcome prevention. They are evaluated based upon whether their recognition, reassessment, escalation, communication, intervention, and clinical decision-making remained reasonably consistent with accepted standards during the actual sequence of care.

Two cases may involve similar deterioration timelines yet produce entirely different litigation conclusions depending upon whether the providers responded reasonably to the information available at the time progression unfolded.

The next pillar examines how clinical obligations are evaluated within the context of evolving deterioration, how provider decisions are analyzed against accepted standards, how reassessment and escalation responsibilities are interpreted, and how breach analysis ultimately becomes separated from retrospective emotional outcome evaluation.

Because before litigation can determine whether care fell below the standard, the progression must first be reconstructed clearly enough to evaluate what was reasonably knowable during the actual sequence itself.

And in medical litigation, liability depends not upon perfect outcome prevention, but upon whether the response remained reasonable within the context of the information available before the outcome was known.

CHAPTER - 04

STANDARD OF CARE REVIEW

Evaluating whether the standard of care was maintained.

This chapter establishes a foundational pillar within the Lexcura Clinical Intelligence Model™ creating the evidentiary framework required for defensible medical-legal analysis.

EVALUATING CLINICAL OBLIGATIONS WITHIN REAL-TIME CONDITIONS

At intake, the allegations appeared straightforward.

A 68-year-old female presented to the emergency department with worsening shortness of breath, tachycardia, fever, hypotension, and increasing confusion following several days of progressive respiratory illness. Initial nursing assessments documented abnormal vital signs, elevated respiratory rate, declining oxygen saturation, and concern regarding possible sepsis progression shortly after arrival.

Over the following several hours, the patient's condition continued deteriorating.

Repeated reassessments documented worsening respiratory distress, increasing oxygen requirements, persistent hypotension, declining urine output, and progressive mental status changes. Nursing staff documented repeated concerns regarding instability and physician notification throughout portions of the progression.

Approximately seven hours after arrival, the patient suffered respiratory failure requiring emergency intubation and ICU transfer before later developing septic shock and multi-organ dysfunction.

The family believed the deterioration should have been recognized much earlier. The attorney initially agreed.

At first review, the chronology appeared highly concerning. The records suggested delayed escalation, prolonged instability, and narrowing intervention opportunity before definitive treatment ultimately occurred.

But as the analysis progressed, another question became central:

Given what was reasonably knowable during the progression itself, did the providers respond in a manner consistent with accepted standards of care?

That distinction forms the foundation of Standard of Care Review within the Lexcura Clinical Intelligence Model™.

Because poor outcome alone does not establish breach.

A patient may suffer catastrophic deterioration despite appropriate care. Conversely, deviation from accepted standards may occur even before irreversible injury becomes fully apparent.

Litigation therefore cannot evaluate provider conduct solely through retrospective outcome.

The analysis must evaluate the clinical obligations that reasonably existed during the actual progression itself.

Standard of Care Review examines whether recognition, reassessment, escalation, communication, intervention, monitoring, documentation, and clinical decision making remained reasonably consistent with what similarly trained providers would have been expected to do under comparable circumstances.

This distinction is critically important because medical litigation does not evaluate perfection. It evaluates reasonableness within real-time clinical conditions.

Providers are not expected to possess hindsight knowledge of the final outcome while care is unfolding. They are expected to recognize clinically significant deterioration, respond appropriately to evolving instability, reassess changing conditions, escalate when necessary, and act within accepted standards based upon the information reasonably available at the time decisions were being made.

This is why Standard of Care Review depends heavily upon the earlier pillars within the Lexcura Clinical Intelligence Model™.

Record Integrity must first establish whether the sequence can be reconstructed reliably. Baseline Profiling must determine the patient's physiologic reserve and recovery potential. Timeline Reconstruction must identify when deterioration became sufficiently recognizable to create meaningful escalation opportunity.

Only then can Standard of Care Review evaluate whether the response itself remained clinically reasonable within the context of the progression that actually existed.

Because before litigation can determine whether care fell below accepted standards, the clinical sequence must first establish what providers reasonably knew, when they knew it, and what obligations emerged as the deterioration progressed.

| *Defining* Standard Of Care Review

Within the Lexcura Clinical Intelligence Model™, Standard of Care Review refers to the structured evaluation of whether clinical decision-making, reassessment, escalation, communication, intervention, and overall management remained reasonably consistent with accepted professional standards during the actual progression of care.

The purpose of Standard of Care Review is not to determine whether a better outcome might theoretically have been possible.

It is to evaluate whether similarly trained providers, functioning under comparable clinical conditions and possessing the same information reasonably available at the time, would likely have responded differently.

This distinction becomes critically important in medical litigation because poor outcome alone does not establish negligence.

A patient may deteriorate despite appropriate care. A catastrophic injury may occur despite timely intervention. Medicine frequently involves uncertainty, competing diagnoses, evolving presentation, and rapidly changing physiologic conditions that must be managed in real time rather than with retrospective clarity.

Standard of Care Review therefore cannot evaluate clinical conduct through hindsight alone. It must evaluate how providers responded to the progression that was actually visible during the sequence itself.

This includes evaluating whether warning signs were recognized appropriately, whether reassessment occurred within reasonable intervals, whether escalation obligations were identified, whether communication between providers remained adequate, whether intervention timing remained reasonable, and whether clinical decision-making reflected accepted standards under the circumstances that existed at the time.

Importantly, Standard of Care Review does not evaluate perfection.

Medicine is not an exact science, and providers are not expected to predict every outcome with certainty. Litigation instead evaluates whether the response remained clinically reasonable within the context of the information reasonably available before the final outcome became known.

Two patients may ultimately experience similar catastrophic injuries while producing entirely different Standard of Care conclusions.

In one case, providers may recognize deterioration promptly, escalate appropriately, reassess consistently, communicate effectively, and intervene within accepted standards despite the patient ultimately suffering irreversible decline.

In another, delayed reassessment, missed escalation opportunity, inadequate communication, incomplete monitoring, or failure to respond appropriately to worsening instability may substantially alter the litigation analysis.

The outcomes may appear similar superficially.

The clinical reasonableness of the response may be profoundly different.

This is why Standard of Care Review serves as one of the central analytical pillars within the Lexcura Clinical Intelligence Model™.

Because before litigation can determine whether breach occurred, the progression must first establish what providers reasonably knew, what obligations emerged from that information, and whether the response remained consistent with accepted standards during the actual sequence of care.

The Difference Between Bad Outcome And Breach

One of the most important principles in medical litigation is understanding that poor outcome and breach of the standard of care are not automatically the same thing.

This distinction is foundational to Standard of Care Review.

Patients may experience catastrophic deterioration despite appropriate medical management. Severe complications may occur despite timely intervention, proper reassessment, appropriate escalation, and reasonable clinical decision-making throughout the progression of care.

Medicine does not guarantee outcome.

It requires providers to respond reasonably to the information available at the time decisions are being made.

Medical litigation often creates unrealistic retrospective expectations because retrospective review naturally creates emotional pressure to equate severe injury with negligence. Families may believe the outcome "must have been preventable" because the deterioration ultimately became catastrophic. Attorneys may initially view devastating injury as evidence that something necessarily went wrong. Even experts may feel drawn toward retrospective assumptions once the final outcome is known.

But Standard of Care Review must separate emotional outcome from clinical obligation. The analytical question is not whether the outcome was tragic.

The question is whether providers recognized, reassessed, escalated, communicated, monitored, and intervened in a manner reasonably consistent with accepted standards during the actual progression itself.

A patient with overwhelming sepsis, advanced hemorrhage, severe neurologic injury, or rapidly progressive multi-organ failure may deteriorate despite aggressive and appropriate care.

Conversely, a patient with initially reversible instability may experience avoidable decline if warning signs are missed, reassessment is delayed, escalation obligations are not recognized, or intervention opportunity is lost during the progression.

This is why Standard of Care Review cannot begin with the outcome alone. It must begin with the clinical sequence.

Because in medical litigation, devastating injury may strengthen emotional reaction, but emotional reaction alone does not establish breach.

Breach depends upon whether the response remained clinically reasonable within the context of the information reasonably available before the outcome was known.

The Role Of Real-Time Clinical Judgment

One of the most difficult aspects of Standard of Care Review is recognizing that providers make decisions within evolving clinical conditions rather than through retrospective certainty.

Medical care unfolds in real time.

Clinicians are often required to evaluate incomplete information, changing presentation, competing diagnoses, fluctuating vital signs, evolving laboratory findings, and uncertain progression while simultaneously making reassessment, escalation, communication, and intervention decisions under significant time pressure.

This distinction becomes critically important in litigation because retrospective review naturally creates a far clearer picture of the progression than providers possessed during the actual sequence itself.

Once catastrophic outcome occurs, the chronology often appears linear and obvious in hindsight. Warning signs that later seem unmistakable may initially have emerged gradually, inconsistently, or within a broader clinical picture containing competing explanations and overlapping comorbidities.

Standard of Care Review must therefore evaluate what providers reasonably knew at the time decisions were being made rather than what later became obvious after the outcome was known.

This does not eliminate accountability.

Providers are still expected to recognize clinically significant deterioration, respond appropriately to evolving instability, reassess changing conditions, escalate when necessary, and intervene within accepted standards as the progression unfolds.

But litigation must evaluate those obligations within the context of real-time clinical judgment rather than retrospective certainty.

A provider managing early sepsis, internal hemorrhage, neurologic decline, or progressive respiratory compromise may initially face incomplete or evolving clinical information before the full severity of deterioration becomes apparent. The question is not whether the final outcome eventually became obvious.

The question is whether the provider's response remained clinically reasonable based upon the information reasonably identifiable during the progression itself.

This is one of the most important distinctions within the Lexcura Clinical Intelligence Model™.

Because Standard of Care Review evaluates clinical judgment within the uncertainty that existed before the outcome was known - not within the clarity created afterward.

Reasonableness Under Clinical Conditions

One of the central principles of Standard of Care Review is that providers are evaluated according to what was clinically reasonable under the conditions that actually existed during the progression of care.

This distinction is critically important because medical litigation often creates unrealistic retrospective expectations once catastrophic outcome becomes known.

After severe deterioration occurs, it may appear that providers should have recognized every warning sign immediately, escalated without delay, selected the correct diagnosis instantly, and prevented the outcome entirely. Yet real-world clinical care rarely unfolds with that level of clarity.

Providers frequently manage incomplete information, evolving symptoms, competing diagnoses, fluctuating reassessment findings, changing physiologic conditions, and uncertain progression while simultaneously making treatment decisions under significant time pressure.

Standard of Care Review therefore cannot evaluate isolated decisions outside the context in which they were made.

The analysis must examine whether the provider's actions remained reasonably consistent with accepted standards given the information reasonably available at that specific point in the progression.

A provider may ultimately select an incorrect diagnosis while still acting reasonably based upon the presentation that existed at the time. Conversely, a provider may possess increasingly obvious warning signs of deterioration yet fail to respond appropriately as the progression evolves.

This distinction substantially alters litigation analysis.

Because medicine does not require perfect outcome prediction.

It requires providers to respond reasonably to recognizable clinical risk as it emerges during the actual sequence of care.

Two providers may manage similar patients differently while both remaining within accepted standards depending upon the clinical circumstances, available information, evolving reassessment findings, institutional resources, and progression visible during the sequence itself.

This is why Standard of Care Review focuses heavily on context.

The issue is not whether a different decision might theoretically have been possible in hindsight.

The issue is whether the provider's actual response remained clinically reasonable within the conditions that existed before the final outcome became known.

Because in medical litigation, breach is determined not by retrospective perfection, but by whether the response departed meaningfully from accepted standards under real-time clinical conditions.

The Danger Of Retrospective Standard Elevation

One of the greatest analytical dangers in medical litigation is retrospective standard elevation.

Once catastrophic outcome occurs, there is a natural tendency to raise expectations regarding what providers "should have known," "should have recognized," or "should have prevented" during the progression itself.

This distortion develops because hindsight creates clarity that did not fully exist in real time.

After severe deterioration, warning signs that initially appeared subtle, evolving, intermittent, or clinically ambiguous may later seem unmistakable once the final outcome becomes known.

Decisions that were made under uncertainty may retrospectively appear unreasonable simply because the progression ultimately ended badly.

Standard of Care Review must guard carefully against this distortion.

Providers are not evaluated according to whether they achieved perfect outcome prevention. They are evaluated according to whether their recognition, reassessment, escalation, communication, monitoring, and intervention remained reasonably consistent with accepted standards under the conditions that actually existed during the sequence of care.

This distinction becomes critically important because medicine frequently involves incomplete information, competing diagnostic possibilities, evolving presentation, and fluctuating physiologic findings.

A provider evaluating early sepsis, occult hemorrhage, neurologic decline, pulmonary embolism, or progressive respiratory compromise may initially encounter subtle abnormalities before the full severity of deterioration becomes clinically obvious.

Retrospective review often compresses that uncertainty.

Once the catastrophic outcome is known, earlier findings may appear far more significant than they reasonably appeared during the actual progression itself.

Standard of Care Review therefore cannot impose obligations that only became obvious after the final outcome occurred.

The analysis must remain anchored to what was reasonably identifiable during the sequence itself.

This does not eliminate accountability when providers fail to recognize clinically actionable deterioration or depart meaningfully from accepted standards.

But it does require litigation analysis to separate reasonable clinical uncertainty from true deviation in care.

Because in medical litigation, breach cannot be established by elevating the standard retrospectively after the outcome is already known.

Recognizing Actionable Deterioration

One of the most important components of Standard of Care Review is determining when deterioration progressed from clinical observation into actionable clinical risk.

This distinction is rarely as simple as it appears in hindsight.

Patients frequently demonstrate isolated abnormalities that may not independently require immediate escalation. Mild tachycardia, transient hypotension, intermittent oxygen desaturation, low-grade fever, or temporary confusion may initially appear clinically manageable depending upon the broader context of the patient's presentation.

Standard of Care Review therefore cannot evaluate isolated findings alone. The analysis must evaluate how the overall progression evolved over time.

A patient's condition may initially appear relatively stable before progressively developing a recognizable pattern of worsening instability through escalating oxygen requirements, declining urine output, increasing respiratory distress, worsening laboratory abnormalities, altered mental status, persistent hypotension, or repeated reassessment concerns.

At some point during that progression, the clinical picture may become sufficiently concerning that reassessment obligations, escalation responsibilities, additional intervention, or higher-level evaluation become reasonably necessary.

Determining when that transition occurred is often central to litigation analysis.

This is where Standard of Care Review intersects closely with Timeline Reconstruction.

Timeline Reconstruction establishes when deterioration became identifiable.

Standard of Care Review evaluates whether the response to that deterioration remained clinically reasonable.

These are not identical questions.

A provider may recognize worsening instability appropriately yet still respond reasonably under the circumstances. Conversely, deterioration may become sufficiently actionable that failure to reassess, escalate, monitor, communicate, or intervene appropriately begins departing from accepted standards.

This distinction fundamentally shapes breach analysis.

Because in medical litigation, the issue is not whether abnormalities eventually existed.

The issue is when the progression became sufficiently actionable that accepted standards reasonably required a different clinical response.

The Difference Between Error In Judgment And Deviation From Standard

One of the most misunderstood concepts in medical litigation is the distinction between an unfavorable clinical decision and a true deviation from the standard of care.

Medicine frequently requires judgment within evolving clinical conditions. Providers must often make decisions where multiple reasonable approaches may exist simultaneously. Diagnostic uncertainty, incomplete information, competing clinical priorities, fluctuating reassessment findings, and rapidly changing physiologic conditions may all influence how treatment decisions unfold during the progression of care.

For this reason, not every imperfect decision constitutes negligence.

A provider may ultimately select a less effective treatment strategy, pursue a diagnosis that later proves incorrect, or fail to predict the eventual severity of deterioration while still acting within the range of clinically reasonable judgment under the circumstances that existed at the time.

Standard of Care Review therefore cannot evaluate medical decision-making through outcome alone.

The analysis must determine whether the provider's conduct departed meaningfully from what similarly trained clinicians reasonably would have done under comparable clinical conditions.

This distinction becomes important because retrospective review naturally creates pressure to interpret any unfavorable outcome as evidence of error.

Once catastrophic injury occurs, alternative decisions often appear obvious in hindsight.

Attorneys, families, and even experts may begin focusing on what "should have been done differently" after the final outcome becomes known.

But the existence of a different possible decision does not automatically establish breach.

The central issue is whether the provider's actual response remained within the range of clinically acceptable judgment during the progression itself.

A provider who reasonably evaluates available information, reassesses evolving conditions, responds to recognizable deterioration, and acts within accepted clinical standards may still experience poor patient outcome despite appropriate care.

Conversely, a provider who ignores actionable instability, fails to reassess worsening progression, delays necessary escalation, or departs substantially from accepted management may create meaningful deviation even before catastrophic injury ultimately develops.

This is why Standard of Care Review evaluates reasonableness rather than perfection. Because in medical litigation, breach is not established merely because another decision might have been possible.

It is established when the provider's conduct falls meaningfully outside the range of clinically acceptable judgment under the conditions that actually existed during the sequence of care.

Communication Failure And Standard Of Care

One of the most important components of Standard of Care Review is evaluating how communication functioned during the progression of deterioration.

In many medical negligence cases, the central issue is not the complete absence of clinical concern.

The issue is whether worsening instability was communicated clearly, escalated appropriately, acknowledged adequately, and acted upon within a reasonable timeframe as the patient's condition evolved.

This distinction becomes important because modern healthcare is rarely managed by a single provider functioning in isolation.

Patient care frequently involves multiple nurses, physicians, consultants, therapists, rapid response teams, shift changes, handoffs, and interdisciplinary communication pathways occurring simultaneously throughout the progression of care.

As a result, clinically significant deterioration may become visible to one provider before it is fully appreciated by another.

Standard of Care Review therefore examines not only whether deterioration existed, but whether communication surrounding that deterioration remained reasonably effective as instability progressed.

A nurse may appropriately recognize worsening hypotension, escalating oxygen requirements, declining mental status, or increasing respiratory distress. Yet if communication to the responsible provider becomes delayed, incomplete, unclear, undocumented, or insufficiently escalated, meaningful intervention opportunity may narrow rapidly despite early recognition of instability itself.

Conversely, providers may receive communication regarding concerning changes while still responding reasonably within the context of the information available at the time.

This distinction substantially affects litigation analysis.

Because communication failure does not always arise from one dramatic breakdown. In many cases, deterioration progresses through smaller communication failures occurring repeatedly throughout the sequence, including incomplete handoff, delayed physician notification, unclear escalation language, undocumented reassessment concern, fragmented consultant communication, or failure to appreciate worsening trend progression collectively over time.

Standard of Care Review evaluates whether those communication processes remained reasonably sufficient to support safe clinical management as the patient's condition evolved.

Importantly, the analysis cannot rely solely upon retrospective assumptions regarding what individual providers later claim they understood.

The records must demonstrate how information was communicated during the progression itself.

Because in medical litigation, communication is not evaluated merely by whether concern existed internally.

It is evaluated by whether clinically significant deterioration was communicated clearly enough to support timely recognition, reassessment, escalation, and intervention under the circumstances that actually existed during the sequence of care.

The Role Of Documentation In Standard Of Care Review

Documentation plays a central role in Standard of Care Review because the records often become the primary evidence through which clinical judgment, reassessment, escalation, communication, and intervention are later evaluated.

In medical litigation, providers are frequently judged not only by what actions were performed, but by whether the records can demonstrate what was recognized, when it was recognized, how the patient was reassessed, what concerns were communicated, and why specific decisions were ultimately made during the progression of care.

This distinction becomes critically important because documentation serves multiple functions simultaneously.

It reflects the patient's evolving condition, preserves the chronology of clinical events, communicates information between providers, supports continuity of care, and later becomes the evidentiary foundation upon which litigation analysis is reconstructed.

Strong documentation often strengthens Standard of Care Review substantially.

Clear reassessment findings, accurate vital sign trends, timely escalation notes, documented communication, physician response, differential reasoning, intervention rationale, and progression tracking may all help demonstrate that providers were actively recognizing and responding to evolving instability throughout the sequence itself.

Conversely, weak documentation may significantly destabilize the analysis.

Incomplete reassessments, vague charting, absent escalation documentation, inconsistent timestamps, delayed entries, undocumented communication, or failure to record clinical reasoning may create substantial uncertainty regarding what providers actually recognized during the progression of deterioration.

Importantly, poor documentation does not automatically establish poor care. A provider may respond appropriately while documenting inadequately.

But in litigation, inadequate documentation often weakens the ability to defend the reasonableness of the response because the records can no longer clearly demonstrate what was known, what concerns existed, or how clinical judgment evolved during the sequence itself.

This distinction becomes particularly important during catastrophic cases involving rapid deterioration, escalating instability, communication disputes, or delayed intervention allegations.

Retrospective testimony alone rarely carries the same evidentiary weight as contemporaneous documentation created during the actual progression of care.

Standard of Care Review therefore evaluates not only the clinical actions themselves, but whether the documentation can reliably support the reasonableness of those actions under scrutiny.

Because in medical litigation, providers are often defended through the records long before they are defended through testimony.

CASE ANALYSIS - 1

Clear Deviation from Accepted Standard of Care

A 54-year-old male presented to the emergency department with worsening chest pain, diaphoresis, nausea, tachycardia, and progressive shortness of breath. Initial nursing documentation identified elevated blood pressure, increasing respiratory distress, and persistent chest discomfort radiating into the left arm and jaw.

Electrocardiogram findings demonstrated evolving ischemic changes, and serial cardiac biomarkers revealed progressive elevation consistent with acute myocardial infarction.

Over the following several hours, the patient's condition continued deteriorating.

Repeated nursing reassessments documented worsening pain, increasing diaphoresis, escalating oxygen requirements, and progressive hemodynamic instability. Multiple nursing notes reflected ongoing concern regarding possible evolving cardiac compromise and documented repeated physician notification attempts throughout the progression.

Importantly, the chronology remained highly stable.

The records clearly established when worsening instability became identifiable, when escalation concerns were communicated, and when intervention opportunity remained realistically available before irreversible deterioration occurred.

Despite these findings, definitive cardiology consultation and transfer for intervention were substantially delayed.

The records demonstrated prolonged intervals without reassessment by the responsible provider despite visible progression of instability. Escalation concerns documented by nursing staff were not acted upon promptly, and no alternative diagnostic explanation sufficiently accounted for the worsening presentation during the progression itself.

As Standard of Care Review deepened, the litigation analysis became substantially stronger. This was not simply a case involving poor outcome alone.

The records demonstrated a recognizable pattern of escalating instability that reasonably required more aggressive reassessment, escalation, and intervention under accepted clinical standards.

Importantly, the deviation did not arise solely from one isolated decision.

The breach emerged progressively through delayed reassessment, inadequate escalation response, prolonged intervention delay, and failure to respond appropriately to worsening instability despite increasingly visible clinical deterioration.

This distinction became critically important.

Because the chronology, documentation, communication records, and progression of instability collectively demonstrated that meaningful intervention opportunity likely remained available while the patient's condition was still potentially reversible.

Expert reviewers were therefore able to support breach analysis with greater confidence.

The litigation analysis did not depend heavily upon retrospective speculation or outcome-driven assumption. Instead, the records themselves demonstrated a progression during which accepted standards reasonably required a more urgent response than what ultimately occurred.

As a result, Standard of Care Review substantially strengthened causation sustainability, expert durability, and overall litigation stability.

The strength of the case did not arise solely from the severity of the myocardial infarction.

It arose from the ability to demonstrate that the response to worsening deterioration departed meaningfully from accepted standards during a period when meaningful intervention opportunity still existed.

This is one of the central principles of Standard of Care Review within the Lexcura Clinical Intelligence Model™: Breach is not established by poor outcome alone.

It is established when the clinical response departs meaningfully from accepted standards under the conditions that existed during the actual progression of care.

CASE ANALYSIS - 2

Reasonable Clinical Response Despite Catastrophic Outcome

A 79-year-old female with advanced chronic obstructive pulmonary disease, congestive heart failure, chronic kidney disease, insulin-dependent diabetes, and significant baseline frailty presented to the emergency department with worsening shortness of breath, fever, increasing weakness, and declining oxygen saturation following several days of progressive respiratory illness.

Initial evaluation demonstrated tachycardia, hypotension, elevated respiratory rate, diffuse pulmonary infiltrates, worsening renal dysfunction, and evidence of evolving sepsis with acute respiratory compromise.

Over the following several hours, the patient's condition deteriorated progressively despite aggressive treatment.

The records demonstrated repeated reassessments, timely physician evaluation, escalating oxygen support, broad-spectrum antibiotics, fluid resuscitation, respiratory therapy involvement, serial laboratory monitoring, specialist consultation, and repeated communication between nursing staff and providers throughout the progression itself.

Importantly, the chronology remained highly stable.

The records established when deterioration became identifiable, when escalation obligations emerged, how providers responded to worsening instability, and how intervention decisions evolved during the sequence of care.

Despite these efforts, the patient ultimately developed severe respiratory failure requiring intubation before later progressing to septic shock and multi-organ dysfunction resulting in death several days later.

At intake, the outcome appeared devastating.

The family strongly believed earlier intervention should have prevented the deterioration, and the severity of the final outcome initially created substantial emotional concern regarding possible negligence.

However, deeper Standard of Care Review produced a markedly different analysis.

The records demonstrated that providers recognized worsening instability appropriately, escalated care progressively, reassessed changing conditions consistently, communicated evolving concerns adequately, and intervened within accepted standards throughout the progression itself.

Most importantly, the patient possessed substantial baseline physiologic vulnerability before the deterioration occurred.

Advanced frailty, chronic cardiopulmonary disease, poor reserve, and significant comorbid burden substantially limited reversibility despite aggressive treatment efforts.

As a result, the litigation analysis became increasingly difficult to support from a breach standpoint.

The catastrophic outcome itself did not establish deviation from accepted standards.

Instead, the records demonstrated a clinically reasonable response to a rapidly progressive and physiologically severe condition despite the patient ultimately failing to recover.

This distinction became critically important.

Because Standard of Care Review does not determine whether providers successfully prevented deterioration in every circumstance.

It determines whether the response remained clinically reasonable under the conditions that existed during the actual progression of care.

Expert reviewers were therefore far more cautious regarding breach analysis despite the severity of the patient's death.

The records demonstrated ongoing reassessment, escalation, communication, intervention, and clinical management that remained reasonably consistent with accepted standards throughout the sequence itself.

As a result, causation sustainability weakened, expert disagreement increased, and the overall litigation posture became substantially less stable despite the catastrophic outcome.

This is one of the most important principles within the Lexcura Clinical Intelligence Model™: Severe outcome alone does not establish negligence.

Standard of Care Review must determine whether the clinical response departed meaningfully from accepted standards under the real-time conditions that actually existed during the progression of care.

Applying Standard Of Care Review

Understanding Standard of Care Review conceptually is only the beginning. The true importance of this pillar becomes apparent when the framework is applied within actual litigation analysis.

In practice, Standard of Care Review determines whether providers responded reasonably to recognizable clinical deterioration under the conditions that existed during the progression itself. The analysis evaluates whether reassessment, escalation, communication, intervention, monitoring, and clinical decision-making remained reasonably consistent with accepted standards before the final outcome became known.

The following exercise is designed to apply these principles within a realistic litigation setting.

As you review the scenario, it is important to separate emotional reaction to the outcome from the actual clinical obligations that existed during the sequence of care. Consider how the providers responded to worsening instability, whether escalation obligations became sufficiently actionable, whether reassessment and communication remained appropriate, and whether the records demonstrate a clinically reasonable response within the circumstances that existed at the time.

This distinction is central within the Lexcura Clinical Intelligence Model™.

Because catastrophic outcome alone does not establish breach.

Standard of Care Review must first determine whether the clinical response departed meaningfully from accepted standards under the real-time conditions that existed during the actual progression of care.

Evaluating Clinical Reasonableness During Progressive Deterioration

A 63-year-old male presented to the emergency department with worsening abdominal pain, fever, tachycardia, hypotension, nausea, and increasing confusion following several days of progressive gastrointestinal symptoms.

Initial nursing assessments documented elevated respiratory rate, mild hypotension, increasing abdominal tenderness, elevated white blood cell count, rising lactate levels, and concern regarding possible sepsis progression. Intravenous fluids, broad-spectrum antibiotics, and initial laboratory evaluation were initiated shortly after arrival.

Over the following several hours, the patient's condition fluctuated.

At certain points during the progression, blood pressure improved transiently following fluid administration and oxygen requirements remained relatively stable.

However, repeated reassessments later documented worsening tachycardia, declining urine output, increasing abdominal pain, escalating confusion, and progressively worsening laboratory abnormalities.

Nursing staff documented repeated communication with the responsible provider regarding worsening instability throughout portions of the progression. Additional imaging and surgical consultation were ultimately obtained after further deterioration became apparent.

Approximately nine hours after arrival, the patient developed septic shock secondary to bowel perforation requiring emergency surgery, vasopressor support, prolonged ICU admission, and subsequent multi-organ dysfunction.

At intake, the case appeared highly concerning.

The family strongly believed earlier surgical intervention should have occurred much sooner, and the prolonged progression before operative management initially created substantial concern regarding delayed recognition and failure to escalate appropriately.

However, deeper Standard of Care Review revealed a more complex sequence.

Certain portions of the progression demonstrated temporary stabilization, evolving presentation, and fluctuating reassessment findings before the patient later deteriorated more dramatically.

As part of the Lexcura Clinical Intelligence Model™, your task is to evaluate whether the providers' response remained reasonably consistent with accepted standards during the actual progression of care.

Questions For Analysis

As you evaluate this case, consider not only whether the patient ultimately deteriorated, but whether the providers' response remained clinically reasonable throughout the progression itself.

At what point did the patient's deterioration become sufficiently actionable to require more aggressive reassessment, escalation, or intervention? Consider how the worsening abdominal findings, rising lactate levels, escalating confusion, declining urine output, and evolving instability influenced the providers' clinical obligations over time.

How should the temporary periods of stabilization affect Standard of Care Review? Do transient improvements in blood pressure and oxygenation reasonably support continued observation during portions of the progression, or should the overall trend still have prompted earlier escalation despite intermittent improvement?

To what extent does the chronology support sustainable breach analysis? Can the records establish a clearly identifiable period during which accepted standards reasonably required a different response before septic shock and bowel perforation became fully apparent?

How might retrospective review influence interpretation of the progression? Consider whether the eventual diagnosis and catastrophic deterioration make earlier abnormalities appear more obvious in hindsight than they may have appeared during the actual sequence itself.

As the case progresses, how do communication, reassessment frequency, escalation timing, and documentation affect Standard of Care Review? Do the records demonstrate active recognition and management of evolving instability, or do they reveal meaningful failures in reassessment, escalation, or response?

Most importantly, based upon the progression itself, did the providers' actions remain reasonably consistent with accepted standards under the real-time clinical conditions that existed before the final outcome became known?

Answer Key& Analysis

The central analytical issue in this case is not simply whether septic shock and bowel perforation ultimately occurred.

The deeper issue is whether the providers' response remained reasonably consistent with accepted standards during the progression that existed before the full severity of deterioration became clinically obvious.

At first review, the matter appears highly concerning.

The patient demonstrated worsening abdominal pain, rising lactate levels, hypotension, escalating confusion, declining urine output, and progressive instability before ultimately developing septic shock and multi-organ dysfunction. An attorney reviewing the sequence initially may view the chronology as strongly supportive of delayed diagnosis, inadequate escalation, and failure to intervene earlier.

However, deeper Standard of Care Review reveals a more complex progression.

The deterioration did not evolve through one uninterrupted and unmistakable decline. Portions of the sequence demonstrated temporary stabilization following fluid resuscitation, intermittent improvement in blood pressure, and fluctuating reassessment findings before more dramatic deterioration later emerged.

This distinction substantially alters the analysis.

Because Standard of Care Review does not evaluate the progression retrospectively from the final diagnosis alone. It evaluates whether the providers' response remained clinically reasonable based upon the information reasonably identifiable during the actual sequence itself.

Although the records demonstrate worsening instability overall, the chronology may not establish one clearly identifiable moment at which surgical intervention or higher-level escalation became unquestionably required under accepted standards.

Instead, the progression evolved through accumulating abnormalities whose significance became increasingly concerning over time.

As a result, expert interpretation may begin diverging regarding when the providers' obligations materially changed during the progression.

Some experts may conclude that the rising lactate levels, worsening abdominal findings, escalating confusion, and declining urine output collectively required earlier surgical escalation before septic shock fully developed. Others may argue that the fluctuating presentation, temporary stabilization, evolving diagnostic picture, and intermittent response to treatment reasonably supported continued reassessment during earlier portions of the sequence.

This distinction substantially changes the breach analysis.

The issue is no longer simply whether the patient deteriorated.

The issue is whether the providers' response departed meaningfully from accepted standards during a period when the clinical picture had become sufficiently actionable to require a different level of reassessment, escalation, or intervention.

Importantly, this does not necessarily eliminate potential liability. Nor does it diminish the seriousness of the patient's outcome.

But the fluctuating progression may substantially weaken the stability of breach analysis by increasing reliance upon retrospective interpretation rather than clearly identifiable real-time deviation from accepted standards.

This is one of the central principles of Standard of Care Review within the Lexcura Clinical Intelligence Model™: Strong breach analysis depends not only upon catastrophic outcome, but upon the ability to demonstrate that the clinical response departed meaningfully from accepted standards under the real-time conditions that existed during the actual progression of care.

Chapter 4 Takeaways

Standard of Care Review

1. Poor outcome alone does not establish breach.

A patient may experience catastrophic deterioration despite appropriate care. Standard of Care Review evaluates whether the clinical response remained reasonably consistent with accepted standards during the actual progression of care.

2. Standard of care is evaluated within real-time clinical conditions.

Providers are not judged according to retrospective certainty. They are evaluated based upon the information reasonably available while the progression was actively unfolding.

3. Medicine requires reasonableness, not perfection.

Healthcare providers frequently manage evolving symptoms, incomplete information, competing diagnoses, fluctuating reassessment findings, and uncertain progression under significant time pressure. The issue is whether the response remained clinically reasonable under those conditions.

4. Hindsight naturally elevates expectations retrospectively.

Once catastrophic outcome becomes known, earlier abnormalities often appear more obvious than they reasonably appeared during the actual sequence itself. Standard of Care Review must guard against retrospective standard elevation.

5. Actionable deterioration develops progressively.

Isolated abnormalities may not independently require escalation. Standard of Care Review evaluates when the overall pattern of instability became sufficiently concerning that accepted standards reasonably required a different clinical response.

6. Error in judgment is not automatically negligence.

Multiple clinically reasonable approaches may exist simultaneously within complex medical care. Breach occurs when the provider's conduct falls meaningfully outside the range of acceptable clinical judgment under the conditions that existed at the time.

7. Communication is central to patient safety and litigation analysis.

Deterioration may become visible to one provider before it is fully appreciated by another. Standard of Care Review evaluates whether clinically significant instability was communicated, escalated, acknowledged, and acted upon appropriately throughout the progression.

8. Documentation substantially influences breach analysis.

Strong documentation helps demonstrate recognition, reassessment, escalation, communication, and clinical reasoning during the progression itself. Weak documentation may significantly weaken the ability to defend the reasonableness of care under scrutiny.

9. Context determines clinical obligation.

Standard of Care Review cannot evaluate isolated decisions outside the circumstances in which they were made. The analysis must examine how providers responded within the broader context of evolving clinical conditions, available information, and progression visible at the time.

10. Strong breach analysis depends upon more than catastrophic outcome.

This is one of the foundational principles of the Lexcura Clinical Intelligence Model™. Breach is established when the clinical response departs meaningfully from accepted standards under the real-time conditions that existed during the actual progression of care.

Transition To The Next Pillar

Once Standard of Care Review determines whether the clinical response remained reasonably consistent with accepted standards, the next question becomes equally important:

How did regulatory obligations, institutional safeguards, policies, protocols, and system-level responsibilities influence the progression itself?

A provider may recognize deterioration appropriately and still function within a system containing communication failures, staffing limitations, policy deviations, documentation breakdowns, delayed escalation pathways, or institutional processes that substantially affect patient safety during the sequence of care.

This is where the Regulatory & Compliance Overlay becomes critical.

Because medical litigation does not evaluate individual provider conduct in isolation alone.

Healthcare delivery occurs within layered systems involving institutional policies, escalation procedures, staffing structures, communication expectations, documentation requirements, regulatory standards, and operational safeguards designed to support safe patient management throughout the progression of care.

In some cases, providers may act reasonably within a system that itself contains significant structural vulnerabilities. In others, institutional compliance mechanisms may function appropriately even when an individual provider departs from accepted standards during the progression itself.

The next pillar examines how regulatory obligations, institutional protocols, accreditation standards, escalation systems, staffing processes, and operational safeguards influence litigation analysis beyond individual clinical judgment alone.

Because before litigation can fully evaluate how and why deterioration progressed, the analysis must also determine whether the surrounding healthcare system functioned reasonably under the conditions that existed during the actual sequence of care.

And in medical litigation, liability may arise not only from individual clinical decisions, but from the larger institutional environment in which those decisions occurred.

CHAPTER - 05

REGULATORY & COMPLIANCE OVERLAY

Identifying system-level regulatory exposure.

This chapter establishes a foundational pillar within the Lexcura Clinical Intelligence Model™ creating the evidentiary framework required for defensible medical-legal analysis.

EVALUATING SYSTEM FAILURE BEYOND INDIVIDUAL CLINICAL JUDGMENT

At intake, the case appeared to involve a straightforward delay in escalation.

A 72-year-old postoperative patient developed worsening hypotension, increasing confusion, tachycardia, declining urine output, and progressive respiratory distress during the first night following abdominal surgery. Nursing documentation reflected repeated reassessment concerns, worsening vital signs, and escalating instability over several hours before the patient ultimately suffered cardiac arrest requiring emergency ICU transfer.

The family believed the nursing staff failed to recognize the deterioration appropriately.

The attorney initially focused on possible bedside negligence and delayed physician notification.

At first review, the chronology appeared to support those concerns. The records demonstrated prolonged instability, delayed intervention, narrowing escalation opportunity, and worsening physiologic decline before definitive intervention ultimately occurred.

But as the analysis deepened, the litigation framework began shifting in a different direction.

The bedside nurses had documented repeated concerns throughout the progression.

Escalation attempts were present within the record. Staffing assignments revealed unusually high patient ratios during the shift. Several reassessments occurred late.

Escalation protocols appeared inconsistently followed. Rapid response activation criteria may have been met earlier in the sequence, yet activation was delayed.

As the system itself came into focus, the analytical question expanded beyond individual provider conduct alone.

Did the surrounding clinical environment function in a manner reasonably capable of supporting safe patient management during the progression itself?

That distinction forms the foundation of the Regulatory & Compliance Overlay within the Lexcura Clinical Intelligence Model™.

Because medical deterioration rarely occurs within isolated decision-making alone.

Healthcare delivery functions through layered systems involving institutional policies, staffing structures, escalation pathways, communication protocols, reassessment expectations, documentation standards, supervisory oversight, regulatory obligations, and operational safeguards designed to support patient safety throughout the continuum of care.

When those systems function appropriately, they may strengthen recognition, escalation, intervention timing, and continuity of care even during rapidly evolving clinical deterioration.

When those systems weaken, instability may progress despite individual providers attempting to respond appropriately within increasingly compromised operational conditions.

For this reason, medical litigation cannot evaluate bedside conduct alone without also examining the institutional framework surrounding the progression itself.

A provider may function reasonably within a system containing unsafe staffing patterns, fragmented escalation structures, inadequate supervision, delayed response protocols, documentation failures, or operational processes that substantially impair safe clinical management.

Conversely, institutional safeguards may remain entirely appropriate even when an individual provider departs meaningfully from accepted standards during the progression of care.

The Regulatory & Compliance Overlay therefore examines whether the surrounding healthcare system remained reasonably aligned with accepted regulatory expectations, operational safeguards, institutional obligations, and patient safety standards during the actual sequence itself.

Because before litigation can fully determine how and why deterioration progressed, the analysis must also determine whether the healthcare environment itself functioned reasonably under the conditions that existed during the progression of care.

Defining The Regulatory & Compliance Overlay

Within the Lexcura Clinical Intelligence Model™, the Regulatory & Compliance Overlay refers to the structured evaluation of how institutional policies, staffing systems, escalation pathways, regulatory obligations, accreditation standards, and operational processes influenced the progression of care during the actual clinical sequence itself.

The purpose of this pillar is not simply to identify whether a policy technically existed.

It is to determine whether the healthcare environment functioned in a manner reasonably capable of supporting safe patient management during the progression of care.

This distinction becomes important because medical litigation often focuses initially upon visible bedside interaction while overlooking the operational conditions surrounding that interaction.

Providers do not function independently from the systems in which care is delivered.

Clinical judgment occurs within institutional structures that influence reassessment frequency, escalation timing, communication pathways, documentation expectations, staffing assignments, supervisory oversight, response activation, chain-of-command procedures, and continuity of care throughout the sequence itself.

For this reason, the Regulatory & Compliance Overlay examines whether the surrounding healthcare framework strengthened or weakened the ability to recognize deterioration, communicate instability, escalate concerns, intervene appropriately, and maintain patient safety during the progression of care.

In some matters, institutional systems function appropriately while an individual provider departs meaningfully from accepted standards.

In others, providers may attempt to respond reasonably while functioning inside operational conditions containing unsafe staffing ratios, fragmented escalation structures, inadequate supervision, deficient protocols, documentation failures, or broader organizational instability that substantially impair safe clinical management. This distinction materially alters litigation analysis.

The progression of deterioration may sometimes reflect not only individual clinical decision-making, but also the operational reliability of the healthcare environment itself.

Importantly, the Regulatory & Compliance Overlay does not evaluate healthcare systems according to idealized perfection.

Hospitals, long-term care facilities, rehabilitation centers, outpatient systems, and clinical organizations frequently function under operational strain, fluctuating census, staffing limitations, resource constraints, and rapidly evolving patient acuity.

The analysis instead evaluates whether institutional safeguards and operational processes remained reasonably sufficient to support safe patient care during the progression itself.

This includes examining whether staffing remained appropriate, whether escalation pathways functioned adequately, whether communication structures remained effective, whether reassessments occurred appropriately, whether documentation systems supported continuity of care, and whether institutional protocols reasonably addressed the risks visible during the sequence.

This is why the Regulatory & Compliance Overlay serves as one of the central analytical pillars within the Lexcura Clinical Intelligence Model™.

Because before litigation can fully determine why deterioration progressed, the analysis must evaluate not only what individual providers did, but whether the surrounding healthcare environment functioned reasonably during the actual progression of care.

The Difference Between Policy Existence And Policy Function

One of the most important distinctions within the Regulatory & Compliance Overlay is understanding that the mere existence of a policy does not necessarily establish that the system functioned safely during the progression of care.

Healthcare institutions frequently maintain policies addressing escalation procedures, rapid response activation, reassessment frequency, documentation standards, chain-of-command obligations, staffing expectations, communication protocols, and patient safety requirements.

On paper, these systems may appear entirely appropriate.

Yet litigation often reveals a substantial difference between formal policy existence and operational policy function during real-world clinical conditions.

A facility may maintain a rapid response policy requiring escalation for worsening hypotension, declining oxygen saturation, altered mental status, or progressive instability. However, if staff are inadequately trained, escalation culture discourages activation, physician response remains delayed, staffing ratios impair reassessment frequency, or communication pathways function inconsistently, the policy itself may provide little meaningful protection during actual deterioration.

This distinction becomes significant because regulatory compliance is not evaluated solely through written documentation.

The deeper question is whether the institutional systems functioned reliably enough to support safe patient management during the progression itself.

In some matters, healthcare organizations possess appropriate policies that are inconsistently implemented, poorly enforced, inadequately supervised, or operationally unrealistic under actual staffing and workload conditions.

In others, providers may technically violate institutional policy while still responding reasonably under emergent clinical circumstances requiring rapid judgment beyond rigid procedural structure.

The Regulatory & Compliance Overlay therefore evaluates not only what institutional policies required, but whether those policies remained operationally functional within the real-world conditions surrounding the progression of care.

This includes evaluating whether escalation systems functioned appropriately, whether reassessment expectations remained realistically achievable, whether operational structures supported policy compliance, and whether institutional culture strengthened or weakened patient safety throughout the progression itself. Importantly, healthcare litigation cannot assume that policy language alone accurately reflects bedside operational reality.

A policy may exist formally while repeatedly failing operationally during actual patient deterioration.

Conversely, an institution may function safely and reasonably despite isolated documentation inconsistencies or minor procedural deviation.

This distinction substantially alters institutional liability analysis.

Because in medical litigation, the central issue is not merely whether a policy was written.

The issue is whether the healthcare system functioned in a manner reasonably capable of supporting safe patient care during the actual progression of deterioration.

The Role Of Staffing In System-Level Failure

One of of the most significant factors within the Regulatory & Compliance Overlay is the effect staffing conditions may have on patient safety during the progression of care.

In many medical negligence cases, deterioration does not occur solely because one provider fails to recognize instability appropriately.

The progression may instead develop within operational conditions where staffing limitations impair reassessment frequency, escalation responsiveness, communication efficiency, documentation continuity, supervisory oversight, and overall workload management throughout the sequence itself.

This distinction becomes important because healthcare systems are designed with the assumption that providers possess sufficient time, support, and operational capacity to recognize and respond appropriately to evolving deterioration.

When staffing conditions become excessively strained, those assumptions may begin to fail.

A nurse responsible for an unsafe patient assignment may experience delayed reassessment intervals, fragmented monitoring, incomplete documentation, delayed physician communication, missed trend recognition, or narrowed escalation opportunity despite attempting to manage the assignment appropriately under increasingly difficult conditions.

Similarly, physicians, rapid response teams, respiratory therapists, supervisors, and ancillary staff may all function under operational overload that substantially affects response timing and continuity of care during active deterioration.

The Regulatory & Compliance Overlay therefore examines whether staffing structures remained reasonably capable of supporting safe patient management throughout the progression itself.

This includes evaluating staffing adequacy, acuity burden, supervisory availability, workload distribution, escalation support, and whether operational demands reasonably allowed providers to meet expected reassessment and intervention obligations during the sequence of care.

Importantly, staffing analysis does not assume that every adverse outcome occurring during high workload conditions automatically establishes institutional negligence.

Healthcare systems frequently function under fluctuating census, resource limitations, and rapidly evolving patient acuity.

The analysis instead evaluates whether staffing conditions deteriorated to a level that meaningfully impaired the institution's ability to maintain reasonably safe clinical operations during the progression itself.

This distinction substantially affects litigation analysis.

Because in some matters, providers may appear individually deficient when functioning inside operational conditions that were themselves structurally unsafe.

In other cases, staffing conditions may remain entirely reasonable while individual providers nevertheless depart meaningfully from accepted standards despite adequate institutional support.

The Regulatory & Compliance Overlay therefore examines not only individual provider conduct, but whether the surrounding operational environment reasonably supported safe clinical care during the actual progression of deterioration.

Because in medical litigation, system failure may sometimes emerge not from one isolated clinical decision, but from cumulative operational strain impairing the healthcare system's ability to function safely as deterioration unfolds.

The Difference Between Individual Error And System Failure

One of the most important distinctions within the Regulatory & Compliance Overlay is determining whether deterioration resulted primarily from isolated provider deviation or from broader system-level operational failure.

This distinction is rarely simple.

In many medical negligence cases, litigation initially focuses on the visible bedside provider directly involved in the progression itself. A nurse may appear to have delayed escalation. A physician may appear to have responded slowly. A reassessment may appear incomplete. A rapid response activation may appear delayed.

At first review, the sequence may appear attributable to individual clinical failure alone.

However, deeper system analysis often reveals a more complex operational environment surrounding the progression.

The bedside provider may have been functioning within unsafe staffing conditions, fragmented escalation structures, delayed supervisory response systems, inconsistent chain-of-command enforcement, inadequate orientation, incomplete policy implementation, communication overload, or operational processes that substantially impaired safe clinical management during the deterioration itself.

This distinction becomes important because healthcare systems are designed to function through multiple overlapping safeguards rather than through isolated provider perfection alone.

Safe clinical environments typically depend upon reliable escalation pathways, functional communication systems, adequate staffing support, supervisory oversight, timely provider response, and operational processes capable of identifying worsening instability before catastrophic deterioration occurs.

When multiple safeguards weaken simultaneously, deterioration may progress despite individual providers attempting to function reasonably within increasingly compromised conditions.

Conversely, institutional systems may remain entirely appropriate while one provider independently departs substantially from accepted standards despite adequate support, supervision, staffing, and escalation resources being fully available.

The Regulatory & Compliance Overlay therefore evaluates how operational conditions influenced the progression itself rather than automatically assigning failure to the most visible provider within the chronology.

Importantly, system failure does not eliminate individual accountability.

Nor does individual error automatically eliminate institutional responsibility. Both may coexist simultaneously within the same progression of care.

An institution may maintain unsafe staffing conditions while an individual provider also fails to recognize actionable deterioration appropriately. A physician may delay escalation while communication structures simultaneously fail to support timely reassessment. Supervisory systems may remain inadequate while bedside documentation also becomes fragmented during worsening instability.

This is why system-level litigation analysis requires layered evaluation rather than isolated blame assignment.

Because in medical litigation, deterioration often progresses through interacting operational failures occurring across multiple levels of the healthcare environment simultaneously.

The Regulatory & Compliance Overlay therefore examines whether the surrounding institutional system functioned reasonably enough to support safe patient care during the actual progression itself - not merely whether one provider within that system later became the focus of retrospective scrutiny.

The Role Of Escalation Pathways In Patient Safety

One of the most important operational safeguards within healthcare systems is the presence of effective escalation pathways capable of responding appropriately to clinical deterioration.

In many medical negligence cases, deterioration does not progress because warning signs were entirely absent.

The progression instead reflects failures in how those warning signs were escalated, communicated, acknowledged, and acted upon throughout the sequence of care.

This point becomes important because healthcare systems are designed around the assumption that evolving instability will trigger progressively higher levels of evaluation, supervision, and intervention before irreversible deterioration occurs.

Escalation pathways function as one of the primary safety mechanisms intended to interrupt progressive clinical decline.

When these systems function appropriately, bedside concerns can move rapidly through physicians, supervisors, specialists, rapid response teams, intensivists, or chain-of-command structures capable of mobilizing higher-level intervention as deterioration becomes increasingly actionable.

When escalation systems weaken, intervention delays may develop despite providers recognizing that the patient's condition is deteriorating.

A nurse may repeatedly communicate concern regarding hypotension, respiratory distress, declining mental status, worsening laboratory abnormalities, or escalating oxygen requirements, yet the escalation process itself may become delayed, fragmented, minimized, or operationally ineffective before definitive intervention occurs.

Similarly, physician-to-physician escalation, consultant response systems, supervisory review, rapid response activation, and interdisciplinary communication structures may all influence whether deterioration is addressed promptly during the progression itself.

The Regulatory & Compliance Overlay therefore examines whether escalation systems remained reasonably functional during the sequence of care.

This includes evaluating how escalation obligations were communicated, whether concerns were acknowledged appropriately, whether chain-of-command procedures functioned effectively, whether response timing remained reasonable, and whether institutional culture strengthened or weakened escalation reliability during active deterioration.

Importantly, escalation analysis does not assume that every delayed response automatically establishes system failure.

Healthcare providers frequently manage competing emergencies, fluctuating acuity, uncertain diagnoses, and evolving clinical conditions that may complicate escalation timing during active patient care.

The analysis instead evaluates whether escalation pathways remained reasonably capable of supporting patient safety during the progression itself.

This distinction substantially alters litigation analysis.

Because in some matters, bedside providers may appropriately recognize deterioration while the escalation system surrounding them fails to mobilize adequate response before irreversible decline develops.

In others, escalation systems may remain entirely appropriate while providers fail to utilize those systems despite increasingly actionable instability.

The Regulatory & Compliance Overlay therefore examines not only whether deterioration existed, but whether the institutional escalation structure functioned reliably enough to support safe clinical management during the actual progression of care.

Because in medical litigation, catastrophic deterioration may sometimes reflect not merely missed recognition, but failure of the healthcare system's escalation mechanisms to respond effectively as instability evolved.

The Role Of Institutional Culture In Clinical Deterioration

One of the most difficult aspects of the Regulatory & Compliance Overlay is evaluating how institutional culture influences clinical decision-making during the progression of deterioration.

Unlike staffing ratios, escalation policies, or written protocols, institutional culture is often less visible within the records themselves.

Yet culture may substantially affect how providers recognize instability, communicate concern, escalate deterioration, activate chain-of-command procedures, document reassessment findings, and respond to worsening clinical conditions throughout the sequence of care.

This distinction is important because healthcare systems do not function through policies alone.

They function through the operational behaviors those policies produce within real world clinical environments.

An institution may formally maintain strong escalation procedures while simultaneously developing an operational culture that discourages aggressive escalation, minimizes bedside concerns, delays supervisory involvement, or creates hesitation regarding rapid response activation and physician notification.

In these environments, providers may technically possess the authority to escalate concerns while operational pressure subtly discourages use of those safeguards during active deterioration.

A nurse may hesitate to activate chain-of-command procedures because prior escalation attempts were dismissed routinely. A provider may delay rapid response activation because escalation culture informally discourages "overreaction."

Supervisory staff may normalize delayed reassessment, excessive workload, incomplete documentation, or communication breakdown as routine operational practice despite increasing patient instability.

Over time, these cultural conditions may substantially weaken the reliability of the healthcare system's safety mechanisms.

The Regulatory & Compliance Overlay therefore examines not only whether institutional safeguards formally existed, but whether the surrounding operational culture realistically supported their effective use during the progression itself.

This may include assessing whether escalation concerns were taken seriously, whether providers felt supported in raising safety issues, whether communication was collaborative or dismissive, whether staffing concerns were normalized, whether chain-of-command systems functioned in practice, and whether leadership reinforced or weakened safe operational behavior during deterioration.

Importantly, institutional culture cannot always be identified through one isolated event.

Culture often becomes visible through repeated operational patterns occurring across the chronology itself, including delayed escalation acceptance, fragmented communication, normalization of unsafe workload, repeated documentation gaps, inconsistent supervisory response, or recurrent operational dysfunction occurring during periods of worsening instability.

This distinction substantially affects litigation analysis.

Because deterioration may sometimes progress not solely through one provider's failure, but through a healthcare environment in which unsafe operational behavior gradually becomes normalized across the system itself.

Conversely, institutions with strong patient safety culture may substantially strengthen early recognition, escalation reliability, interdisciplinary communication, and operational accountability even during rapidly evolving deterioration.

The Regulatory & Compliance Overlay therefore evaluates whether the institutional environment functioned in a manner that strengthened or weakened patient safety during the actual progression of care.

Because in medical litigation, healthcare systems are influenced not only by written policy, but by the operational culture that determines how those policies function under real-world clinical conditions.

The Difference Between Regulatory Noncompliance And Causation

One of the most important distinctions within the Regulatory & Compliance Overlay is understanding that regulatory noncompliance does not automatically establish causation.

Healthcare litigation frequently identifies policy violations, documentation deficiencies, staffing concerns, delayed reassessments, accreditation issues, procedural deviations, or failures to follow institutional protocols during the progression of care.

At first review, these findings may appear highly damaging.

Attorneys, families, and even experts may initially assume that the presence of regulatory or policy noncompliance necessarily proves that the deviation caused the patient's outcome.

However, the relationship between noncompliance and causation is often far more complex. A healthcare organization may violate documentation standards, staffing guidelines, reassessment protocols, or escalation procedures without those deficiencies materially altering the patient's ultimate clinical outcome.

Conversely, relatively small operational failures may become critically important when they directly impair recognition, escalation, communication, reassessment, or intervention timing during a period of evolving instability.

This is important because litigation does not evaluate regulatory deviation in isolation alone.

The deeper analytical question is whether the operational failure materially influenced the progression itself in a way that altered patient management, delayed escalation, narrowed intervention opportunity, or weakened the healthcare system's ability to respond appropriately during the sequence of care.

For example, a hospital may technically violate internal staffing policy while the clinical response nevertheless remains timely, coordinated, and reasonably effective throughout the progression itself. In that circumstance, the staffing deviation may carry limited causation significance despite formal noncompliance.

In another case, delayed reassessment caused by unsafe staffing conditions may substantially impair recognition of worsening sepsis during a critical intervention window, materially affecting escalation timing before definitive treatment ultimately occurs.

Both matters involve operational deviation. Only one may support sustainable causation.

The Regulatory & Compliance Overlay therefore examines not only whether institutional failures existed, but whether those failures materially affected the progression of deterioration itself.

Because healthcare systems are imperfect environments where procedural deviations may occur without necessarily producing patient harm.

Medical litigation instead focuses on whether the identified operational failure meaningfully contributed to delayed recognition, impaired escalation, inadequate intervention, communication breakdown, or progression of injury during the actual sequence of care.

Importantly, regulatory violation alone may still carry substantial significance even when causation remains difficult to establish.

Repeated operational deficiencies may strengthen credibility concerns, support broader institutional scrutiny, weaken defense posture, or demonstrate unsafe systemic conditions despite uncertainty regarding direct physiologic impact in one individual case.

But causation analysis still requires more than identifying operational imperfection alone.

It requires demonstrating that the regulatory or institutional failure materially influenced the clinical progression itself.

Because in medical litigation, not every policy violation causes injury.

The central question is whether the operational failure meaningfully altered the progression of care during the actual sequence of deterioration.

The Role Of Accreditation And Regulatory Standards

Healthcare systems do not operate solely according to internal policy.

Hospitals, long-term care facilities, rehabilitation centers, outpatient systems, and other clinical organizations function within broader regulatory and accreditation frameworks designed to establish minimum operational standards for staffing, escalation, documentation, communication, reassessment, and continuity of care.

These external standards often become highly relevant during medical litigation.

Organizations such as The Joint Commission, Centers for Medicare & Medicaid Services (CMS), state health departments, nursing boards, and other regulatory agencies establish operational expectations intended to support safe clinical management during evolving patient deterioration.

Importantly, these standards do not exist merely as administrative formalities.

They are intended to strengthen the healthcare system's ability to recognize instability, escalate worsening conditions appropriately, maintain operational reliability, and reduce preventable harm during active clinical progression.

The Regulatory & Compliance Overlay therefore examines whether institutional operations remained reasonably aligned with accepted regulatory expectations during the actual sequence of care.

This may include evaluating whether escalation procedures functioned appropriately, whether staffing conditions remained operationally reasonable, whether documentation practices supported continuity of care, and whether institutional processes remained sufficiently reliable during the progression itself.

This distinction becomes important because regulatory standards may sometimes reveal broader operational vulnerabilities that are not immediately visible through bedside chronology alone.

An institution may demonstrate repeated staffing deficiencies, delayed response systems, communication failures, inadequate supervision, or recurring escalation breakdowns that collectively suggest deeper systemic instability beyond one isolated patient event.

Conversely, institutions may remain substantially compliant with accepted regulatory standards even when an individual provider independently departs from accepted clinical obligations during the sequence of care.

The Regulatory & Compliance Overlay therefore does not assume that regulatory compliance automatically eliminates institutional liability.

Nor does regulatory deficiency automatically establish negligence.

The analysis instead evaluates how regulatory alignment or operational deviation influenced the reliability of the healthcare system during the progression itself.

Importantly, regulatory standards frequently establish minimum expectations rather than idealized operational perfection.

Healthcare organizations may remain technically compliant while still functioning within strained operational conditions that weaken patient safety reliability during active deterioration.

Similarly, isolated regulatory deficiencies may exist within otherwise safe and operationally functional systems.

This distinction substantially affects litigation analysis.

Because in medical litigation, regulatory review is not simply about identifying administrative violations.

It is about determining whether the healthcare environment functioned reasonably enough to support safe patient care during the actual progression of deterioration.

CASE ANALYSIS - 1

System-Level Failure Contributing to Clinical Deterioration

A 67-year-old male was admitted following abdominal surgery with initially stable postoperative findings. During the overnight shift, the patient began developing worsening hypotension, increasing tachycardia, declining urine output, escalating abdominal pain, and progressive confusion.

Nursing reassessments documented repeated concern regarding evolving instability throughout portions of the progression. Vital sign abnormalities became increasingly persistent, and several reassessment notes reflected concern regarding possible postoperative deterioration requiring physician evaluation.

At first review, the litigation analysis appeared focused primarily upon bedside nursing management.

The attorney initially questioned whether escalation occurred appropriately and whether the bedside nurse failed to recognize worsening instability in a timely manner.

However, deeper Regulatory & Compliance Overlay analysis revealed a far more complex operational environment.

The nurse assigned to the patient was simultaneously responsible for an unusually high-acuity assignment involving multiple unstable postoperative patients during the same shift.

Documentation reflected delayed reassessment intervals, fragmented charting, repeated workflow interruptions, and delayed supervisory response throughout portions of the deterioration.

Importantly, the nurse did attempt escalation.

The records demonstrated repeated physician notification attempts, documentation of worsening instability, and continued reassessment efforts despite increasingly strained operational conditions.

However, the surrounding system itself appeared increasingly unreliable as the deterioration progressed.

Rapid response activation criteria may have been met earlier in the sequence, yet activation did not occur promptly. Supervisory involvement remained limited, escalation pathways became fragmented, and communication delays compounded as the patient's condition worsened.

As the analysis deepened, the litigation framework shifted substantially.

The central issue no longer involved only whether one provider failed to respond appropriately.

The deeper question became whether the surrounding healthcare system functioned reasonably enough to support safe postoperative monitoring and escalation during the progression itself.

Because the deterioration may not have resulted from one isolated clinical failure alone.

Instead, the progression reflected interacting operational weaknesses involving staffing burden, delayed escalation support, fragmented supervision, impaired reassessment continuity, and operational overload during a critical intervention period.

Importantly, this did not eliminate the need to evaluate individual provider conduct. The bedside response still required analysis regarding reassessment frequency, escalation timing, communication clarity, and recognition of worsening deterioration.

However, the Regulatory & Compliance Overlay demonstrated that the providers were functioning inside an operational environment that may itself have substantially impaired safe clinical management throughout the progression.

As a result, the litigation analysis expanded beyond isolated bedside negligence and toward broader institutional responsibility.

The strength of the case did not arise solely from the severity of the patient's deterioration.

It arose from the ability to demonstrate that the surrounding operational systems may have functioned inadequately during a period when timely reassessment, escalation support, and coordinated intervention remained critically important.

This is one of the central principles of the Regulatory & Compliance Overlay within the Lexcura Clinical Intelligence Model™: Clinical deterioration may sometimes reflect not only individual provider deviation, but broader operational failure within the healthcare system surrounding the progression of care.

CASE ANALYSIS - 2

Regulatory Deviation Without Strong Causation Support

An 84-year-old female resident of a skilled nursing facility was admitted to the hospital with progressive weakness, dehydration, worsening confusion, and declining oral intake following several days of clinical deterioration within the facility.

Initial review of the records revealed multiple regulatory and documentation concerns.

Routine reassessment documentation appeared inconsistent during portions of the resident's decline. Nursing notes contained incomplete hydration monitoring, intermittent vital sign gaps, and delayed physician notification regarding worsening intake and progressive weakness.

Several documentation entries appeared retrospective rather than contemporaneous, and portions of the escalation chronology were fragmented.

At intake, the case appeared highly concerning.

The family strongly believed the facility had failed to monitor the resident appropriately, and the attorney initially viewed the documentation deficiencies as evidence of significant institutional negligence contributing to the patient's deterioration.

However, deeper Regulatory & Compliance Overlay analysis substantially altered the litigation framework.

The resident possessed advanced dementia, severe baseline frailty, chronic renal insufficiency, progressive functional decline, recurrent infection history, and significant long-term physiologic vulnerability before the deterioration occurred.

Importantly, the records also demonstrated that portions of the decline may already have been progressing before the documentation gaps became clinically significant.

Although the facility's reassessment practices and documentation continuity appeared operationally deficient in several respects, the causation analysis became increasingly difficult to sustain with confidence.

The central issue was no longer whether regulatory or documentation deviation existed. The records clearly supported portions of that concern.

The deeper question became whether those operational deficiencies materially altered the resident's clinical outcome in a meaningful and defensible way.

As the analysis progressed, expert interpretation began diverging substantially.

Some reviewers argued that earlier escalation, more aggressive hydration management, improved reassessment continuity, and more timely physician involvement may possibly have improved portions of the resident's progression.

Others concluded that the resident's advanced frailty, severe baseline decline, poor physiologic reserve, and progressive underlying deterioration substantially limited reversibility regardless of whether the facility had operated more consistently during the sequence itself.

This distinction became critically important.

Because the presence of operational deficiency alone did not automatically establish sustainable causation.

The litigation analysis instead depended upon whether the regulatory and documentation failures materially impaired intervention opportunity during a period when meaningful reversibility still realistically existed.

Importantly, the facility's operational weaknesses still carried substantial significance.

The documentation deficiencies weakened institutional credibility, raised concern regarding reassessment reliability, and created broader questions regarding operational oversight and patient safety processes within the facility itself.

However, the Regulatory & Compliance Overlay demonstrated that regulatory noncompliance and sustainable causation are not automatically identical conclusions.

As a result, the litigation posture became substantially more complex.

The case continued to present operational and regulatory concern, yet the ability to establish that those deficiencies probably altered the resident's ultimate outcome remained significantly less certain.

This is one of the central principles of the Regulatory & Compliance Overlay within the Lexcura Clinical Intelligence Model™: Operational failure alone does not automatically establish causation.

The analysis must determine whether the regulatory or institutional deficiency materially influenced the clinical progression during a period when meaningful intervention opportunity still existed.

Applying The Regulatory & Compliance Overlay

Understanding the Regulatory & Compliance Overlay conceptually is only the beginning. The true importance of this pillar becomes apparent when operational systems are evaluated within actual litigation reconstruction.

In practice, this pillar determines whether the healthcare environment itself functioned in a manner reasonably capable of supporting safe patient management during the progression of deterioration. The analysis evaluates whether staffing structures, escalation pathways, reassessment systems, supervisory oversight, documentation processes, communication frameworks, institutional protocols, and operational safeguards remained sufficiently reliable under the conditions that existed during the sequence of care.

The following exercise is designed to apply these principles within a realistic litigation setting.

As you review the scenario, it is important to evaluate not only the conduct of the bedside providers, but also the operational environment surrounding their decisions. Consider whether staffing conditions impaired reassessment continuity, whether escalation pathways functioned appropriately, whether communication systems remained effective, whether institutional safeguards supported timely intervention, and whether the healthcare system itself functioned reliably as the patient's instability progressed.

This distinction is central within the Lexcura Clinical Intelligence Model™.

Because clinical deterioration may sometimes reflect not only individual provider judgment, but the operational reliability of the healthcare system surrounding the progression itself.

Evaluating Operational Failure During Progressive Deterioration

A 71-year-old postoperative patient was admitted to a medical-surgical unit following bowel resection surgery. During the first overnight shift, nursing documentation began reflecting worsening hypotension, increasing tachycardia, declining urine output, escalating abdominal pain, and progressive confusion over several hours.

The bedside nurse documented repeated reassessment concerns and multiple physician notification attempts throughout portions of the progression. However, reassessment intervals became inconsistent as the shift progressed, and portions of the documentation reflected delayed charting occurring retrospectively after periods of worsening instability.

Unit staffing records later demonstrated unusually high patient acuity during the shift, including several unstable postoperative admissions requiring frequent reassessment and escalating interventions simultaneously across the unit.

As the patient's condition worsened, escalation became increasingly fragmented.

Rapid response activation criteria may have been met during portions of the progression, yet activation did not occur until significantly later in the sequence.

Supervisory involvement remained limited throughout much of the deterioration, physician response delays were documented intermittently, and communication between providers became increasingly inconsistent as the patient's instability progressed.

Approximately nine hours after the onset of worsening postoperative deterioration, the patient developed septic shock secondary to an anastomotic leak requiring emergency surgery, ICU transfer, vasopressor support, and prolonged critical care management.

At intake, the case initially appeared focused upon possible bedside nursing delay and physician response concerns.

However, deeper Regulatory & Compliance Overlay analysis raised broader questions regarding whether the surrounding operational systems functioned reasonably enough to support safe postoperative monitoring and escalation during the progression itself.

As part of the Lexcura Clinical Intelligence Model™, your task is to evaluate whether the healthcare environment remained operationally capable of supporting safe patient management during the actual sequence of deterioration.

Questions For Analysis

As you evaluate this case, consider not only whether the patient ultimately deteriorated, but whether the surrounding healthcare system functioned reasonably during the progression itself.

At what point did the patient's deterioration become sufficiently actionable to require more aggressive escalation, supervisory involvement, or higher-level intervention? Consider how the worsening hypotension, declining urine output, escalating abdominal pain, increasing confusion, and progressive postoperative instability influenced the operational obligations of both the bedside providers and the institution as the sequence evolved.

How did staffing conditions affect the progression of care? Did the unusually high acuity assignment substantially impair reassessment continuity, escalation timing, documentation reliability, communication efficiency, or the ability of providers to respond appropriately to worsening instability during the shift?

To what extent did the escalation pathways function effectively during the progression itself? Consider whether rapid response activation, physician notification, supervisory involvement, and interdisciplinary communication remained reasonably sufficient to support timely recognition and intervention as the patient's condition deteriorated.

How should the delayed and fragmented documentation influence the analysis? Do the records demonstrate isolated charting deficiencies alone, or do they suggest broader operational strain affecting continuity of care throughout the progression?

As the case progresses, does the chronology support isolated bedside provider failure, broader system-level operational failure, or a combination of both? Consider whether the deterioration reflects individual deviation, institutional weakness, or interacting failures occurring simultaneously across multiple levels of the healthcare environment.

Most importantly, based upon the progression itself, did the surrounding healthcare system remain reasonably capable of supporting safe postoperative management under the real-time operational conditions that existed before the patient developed septic shock and critical deterioration?

Answer Key& Analysis

The central analytical issue in this case is not simply whether the patient ultimately developed septic shock following postoperative deterioration.

The deeper issue is whether the surrounding healthcare system functioned reasonably enough to support safe reassessment, escalation, communication, and intervention during the progression itself.

At first review, the matter appears highly concerning.

The patient demonstrated worsening hypotension, declining urine output, escalating abdominal pain, progressive confusion, and increasingly unstable postoperative findings over several hours before definitive intervention ultimately occurred. An attorney initially reviewing the chronology may reasonably view the sequence as strongly supportive of delayed escalation and failure to intervene appropriately.

However, deeper Regulatory & Compliance Overlay analysis reveals a far more complex operational environment surrounding the deterioration.

The records demonstrate that the bedside nurse did recognize portions of the worsening instability and repeatedly attempted physician notification throughout the progression. Reassessment concerns were documented, and the chronology supports ongoing recognition that the patient's condition was deteriorating.

At the same time, the operational environment itself appeared increasingly strained.

Staffing records demonstrated unusually high-acuity assignments across the unit, fragmented reassessment continuity, weakened documentation consistency, limited supervisory involvement, and delayed escalation response during portions of the progression.

This distinction substantially alters the litigation analysis.

Because the progression may not reflect one isolated bedside failure alone.

Instead, the deterioration appears to have unfolded within an operational environment where multiple safety mechanisms weakened simultaneously during a critical intervention period.

Rapid response activation may reasonably have occurred earlier. Supervisory escalation may have required greater involvement. Excessive workload conditions may also have impaired continuity of monitoring and delayed coordinated intervention as the patient's condition worsened.

Importantly, this does not automatically eliminate the need to evaluate individual provider conduct.

The bedside response still requires analysis regarding reassessment frequency, escalation persistence, communication clarity, documentation reliability, and recognition of worsening postoperative instability throughout the sequence itself.

However, the chronology also supports substantial concern regarding whether the healthcare system surrounding those providers remained operationally capable of supporting safe postoperative management during the progression.

As a result, the litigation framework becomes layered rather than isolated. The analysis no longer focuses solely upon whether one provider made an incorrect clinical decision.

The deeper question becomes whether interacting operational weaknesses collectively impaired the healthcare system's ability to respond appropriately before irreversible deterioration developed.

This distinction becomes important.

Because in medical litigation, catastrophic deterioration may sometimes reflect cumulative operational failure occurring across multiple levels of the healthcare environment simultaneously rather than one isolated bedside deviation alone.

The Regulatory & Compliance Overlay therefore demonstrates how institutional systems, staffing structures, supervisory processes, and operational safeguards may materially influence whether instability is recognized and managed effectively during the actual progression of care.

This is one of the central principles of the Regulatory & Compliance Overlay within the Lexcura Clinical Intelligence Model™: Healthcare litigation must evaluate not only whether individual providers acted reasonably, but whether the surrounding operational environment functioned reliably enough to support safe patient care during the actual sequence of deterioration.

Chapter 5 *Takeaways*

Regulatory & Compliance Overlay

1. Healthcare systems influence clinical deterioration.

Medical deterioration does not occur within isolated provider decision-making alone. Patient care unfolds within operational systems involving staffing structures, escalation pathways, communication processes, supervisory oversight, documentation expectations, institutional safeguards, and regulatory obligations that collectively influence patient safety throughout the progression of care.

2. Policy existence does not automatically establish operational safety.

A healthcare organization may maintain extensive policies addressing escalation, reassessment, documentation, staffing, and patient safety while still functioning operationally in a manner that weakens those safeguards during real-world clinical deterioration. The analysis must evaluate whether institutional systems functioned reliably during the actual progression itself.

3. *Staffing conditions may substantially affect patient safety.*

Unsafe workload, excessive acuity burden, inadequate staffing support, fragmented coverage, and operational overload may impair reassessment continuity, escalation timing, communication reliability, documentation accuracy, and intervention opportunity during worsening instability.

4. *System failure and individual error are not automatically identical.*

Deterioration may reflect isolated provider deviation, broader operational failure, or interacting weaknesses occurring simultaneously across multiple levels of the healthcare environment. The analysis must evaluate how institutional systems influenced the progression itself rather than assigning isolated retrospective blame alone.

5. *Escalation pathways function as critical safety mechanisms.*

Healthcare systems depend upon reliable escalation structures capable of mobilizing higher-level reassessment, intervention, supervision, and communication as instability progresses. When escalation pathways weaken, meaningful intervention opportunity may narrow despite worsening deterioration becoming clinically visible.

6. *Institutional culture influences operational safety.*

Healthcare systems function not only through written policies, but through the operational culture surrounding escalation, communication, supervisory support, documentation, and patient safety behavior during active clinical deterioration. Unsafe operational culture may substantially weaken otherwise appropriate institutional safeguards.

7. Regulatory noncompliance does not automatically establish causation.

Operational deficiency, documentation failure, staffing deviation, or policy noncompliance may raise substantial institutional concern without necessarily proving that the deficiency materially altered the patient's outcome. Litigation must determine whether the operational failure meaningfully influenced the progression itself.

8. Regulatory and accreditation standards provide operational context.

Organizations such as CMS, The Joint Commission, state regulatory agencies, and institutional oversight bodies establish operational expectations intended to support safe patient management during evolving deterioration. Regulatory analysis helps evaluate whether institutional systems functioned reasonably during the progression of care.

9. System-level analysis requires layered evaluation.

Healthcare deterioration often develops through interacting operational weaknesses involving staffing strain, fragmented escalation, delayed communication, supervisory limitations, documentation instability, and institutional process failure occurring simultaneously throughout the progression itself.

10. Operational reliability substantially influences litigation stability.

This is one of the foundational principles of the Regulatory & Compliance Overlay within the Lexcura Clinical Intelligence Model™. Healthcare litigation must evaluate not only whether individual providers acted reasonably, but whether the surrounding healthcare system functioned reliably enough to support safe patient care during the actual progression of deterioration.

Transition To The Next Pillar

Once the Regulatory & Compliance Overlay evaluates whether the surrounding healthcare system functioned reasonably during the progression of care, the next analytical question becomes even more consequential:

Did the identified deviations, delays, operational failures, or clinical breakdowns materially alter the patient's outcome?

This is where Causation Mapping becomes critical.

Because medical litigation ultimately depends not only upon identifying deterioration, breach, regulatory weakness, or operational instability, but upon determining whether those failures meaningfully changed the patient's clinical trajectory in a defensible and physiologically supportable way.

A provider may depart from accepted standards without materially altering the final outcome. A healthcare system may demonstrate operational weakness while the patient's underlying physiology still limits meaningful reversibility regardless of intervention timing. Conversely, relatively small delays in escalation, communication, reassessment, or intervention may become critically important when meaningful recovery opportunity still exists during the progression itself.

This distinction forms the foundation of causation analysis within the Lexcura Clinical Intelligence Model™.

Because litigation does not evaluate deviation in isolation alone.

It evaluates whether the deviation materially influenced the progression of deterioration during a period when earlier recognition, escalation, intervention, or operational reliability probably would have changed the patient's outcome in a meaningful way.

The next pillar therefore examines how clinical deterioration, physiologic reserve, escalation timing, intervention opportunity, operational reliability, and progression stability intersect to determine whether causation can survive analytical and evidentiary scrutiny.

Because before litigation can determine liability responsibly, the analysis must establish not only that something may have gone wrong, but that the identified failure probably altered the clinical outcome during the actual progression of care.

And in medical litigation, that distinction often determines whether a case remains strategically sustainable or becomes increasingly vulnerable under scrutiny.

The Lexcura Clinical Intelligence Model™

"Regulatory failure may reveal system responsibility, but causation determines whether that failure changed the patient's outcome."

CHAPTER - 06

CAUSATION MAPPING

Determining whether the alleged failure altered outcome.

This chapter establishes a foundational pillar within the Lexcura Clinical Intelligence Model™ creating the evidentiary framework required for defensible medical-legal analysis.

DETERMINING WHETHER THE OUTCOME WAS ACTUALLY ALTERED

At intake, the case appeared devastating.

A 58-year-old patient presented to the emergency department with fever, hypotension, worsening confusion, elevated lactate, tachycardia, and laboratory findings concerning for progressive sepsis. Nursing reassessments documented repeated episodes of instability over several hours before ICU transfer ultimately occurred.

The family believed the delay in escalation caused the patient's death.

The attorney initially focused on delayed antibiotic administration, fragmented reassessment, and prolonged hypotension before vasopressor support was initiated.

At first review, the chronology appeared strongly supportive of causation. The patient deteriorated.

Intervention was delayed.

The outcome was catastrophic.

But as the analysis deepened, the litigation framework became far more complicated.

The patient also possessed severe baseline physiologic vulnerability before the deterioration began. Advanced cirrhosis, chronic renal failure, poorly controlled diabetes, recurrent infection history, severe malnutrition, and progressive multi organ dysfunction substantially limited physiologic reserve before sepsis progression ever developed.

Although portions of the escalation sequence appeared operationally concerning, the deeper analytical question was no longer simply whether delays occurred.

The question became whether earlier intervention probably would have changed the outcome in a meaningful and physiologically supportable way.

That distinction forms the foundation of Causation Mapping within the Lexcura Clinical Intelligence Model™.

Because medical litigation does not ultimately depend only upon identifying deterioration, delay, regulatory deviation, or breach of standard.

It depends upon determining whether the identified failure materially altered the patient's clinical trajectory during a period when meaningful reversibility still realistically existed. This distinction is one of the most difficult aspects of medical litigation.

Medicine frequently contains uncertainty. Multiple physiologic variables often interact simultaneously during active deterioration. Critically ill patients may decline despite appropriate intervention, while some patients survive despite substantial delay or imperfect care.

As a result, causation analysis cannot rely solely upon retrospective outcome comparison.

The fact that a catastrophic outcome occurred does not automatically establish that earlier intervention would probably have prevented it.

Nor does the presence of physiologic vulnerability automatically eliminate causation.

Instead, the analysis must determine how timing, baseline reserve, deterioration progression, intervention opportunity, physiologic reversibility, and clinical trajectory interacted throughout the actual sequence of care.

In some matters, relatively small delays may materially alter the outcome because intervention opportunity remained highly salvageable during the progression itself.

In others, severe baseline illness, advanced physiologic collapse, overwhelming injury burden, or limited reversibility may substantially weaken the ability to establish that earlier intervention probably would have changed the final outcome despite apparent deviation.

For this reason, Causation Mapping evaluates far more than whether deterioration occurred.

It evaluates whether the progression itself supports a defensible physiologic connection between the identified failure and the ultimate outcome.

Because before litigation can sustain causation responsibly, the analysis must determine not merely whether something went wrong, but whether the identified failure probably altered the patient's clinical trajectory during the actual progression of deterioration.

Defining Causation Mapping

Within the Lexcura Clinical Intelligence Model™, Causation Mapping refers to the structured evaluation of whether an identified clinical failure, delay, omission, operational breakdown, or deviation materially altered the patient's outcome during the actual progression of care.

The purpose of this pillar is not simply to identify that deterioration occurred.

It is to determine whether the available medical evidence supports a defensible physiologic connection between the alleged failure and the ultimate injury, decline, or death.

Medical litigation frequently begins with retrospective outcome association. A patient deteriorates.

A delay is identified.

A deviation appears visible within the chronology. The outcome becomes catastrophic. At first review, the sequence may appear causally obvious.

However, deeper causation analysis often reveals a far more complex physiologic reality.

Critically ill patients frequently possess multiple overlapping disease processes, severe baseline vulnerability, limited physiologic reserve, progressive chronic illness, competing risk factors, advanced frailty, or evolving multi-organ instability that may independently influence outcome progression regardless of whether deviations occurred during the sequence itself.

For this reason, Causation Mapping does not evaluate deviation in isolation alone.

The analysis instead examines how timing, baseline physiology, deterioration progression, intervention opportunity, reversibility, treatment responsiveness, and clinical trajectory interacted throughout the actual progression of care.

In some matters, relatively small delays in escalation, reassessment, intervention, imaging, antibiotic administration, airway management, operative response, or specialist involvement may materially alter outcome because meaningful reversibility remained present during the progression itself.

In others, severe underlying illness, overwhelming physiologic collapse, advanced injury burden, delayed presentation, or limited reversibility may substantially weaken the ability to establish that earlier intervention probably would have changed the final outcome in a meaningful way. Medical causation is not established merely by identifying a bad outcome following questionable care.

The analysis must determine whether the identified failure probably altered the patient's clinical trajectory beyond what would otherwise have occurred through the underlying disease process itself.

Importantly, Causation Mapping does not require absolute medical certainty.

Medicine rarely provides absolute certainty, particularly during complex critical deterioration involving multiple interacting physiologic variables.

However, sustainable causation still requires more than theoretical possibility.

The analysis must establish that the alleged deviation more likely than not materially contributed to the progression of injury under the physiologic conditions that existed during the sequence itself.

This is why Causation Mapping serves as one of the central analytical pillars within the Lexcura Clinical Intelligence Model™.

Because before litigation can responsibly attribute liability, the analysis must determine not only whether something may have gone wrong, but whether the identified failure probably changed the patient's outcome during the actual progression of care.

The Difference Between Possibility And Probability

One of the most important distinctions within Causation Mapping is the difference between medical possibility and legal probability.

Medicine frequently operates within possibility.

Clinicians often acknowledge that earlier intervention, different treatment decisions, faster escalation, or more aggressive management may possibly have altered a patient's course. In complex medicine, absolute certainty rarely exists, and multiple theoretical outcomes may remain conceivable even during severe physiologic deterioration.

Litigation, however, applies a far more demanding standard.

The question is not whether earlier intervention could possibly have changed the outcome.

The question is whether the available evidence supports that earlier intervention probably would have changed the outcome in a meaningful and physiologically defensible way.

Retrospective outcome analysis naturally creates emotional and cognitive pressure to associate catastrophic outcomes with preventability.

Families may strongly believe their loved one "would still be alive" if treatment had occurred sooner. Attorneys may initially interpret visible delays as inherently causative. Even experts may feel drawn toward retrospective assumptions when deterioration appears dramatic or intervention opportunities appear delayed within the chronology.

Yet deeper physiologic analysis may substantially complicate those assumptions.

A patient with advanced frailty, severe chronic illness, overwhelming infection, delayed presentation, extensive organ dysfunction, metastatic disease, catastrophic injury burden, or profoundly limited physiologic reserve may still possess theoretical survival possibility despite progressive deterioration.

But theoretical possibility alone does not establish sustainable causation. A patient may have survived.

Earlier intervention may have helped.

More aggressive escalation may have altered portions of the clinical trajectory. However, causation analysis requires more than retrospective possibility.

It requires evidence capable of supporting probability under physiologic and evidentiary scrutiny.

For this reason, Causation Mapping evaluates whether meaningful reversibility realistically remained present during the progression itself.

The analysis examines how baseline reserve, deterioration timing, treatment responsiveness, severity of physiologic collapse, intervention opportunity, and progression stability interacted throughout the sequence of care.

In some matters, the chronology strongly supports that earlier intervention probably would have altered the outcome because deterioration remained highly reversible during the delay period itself.

In others, severe baseline compromise or advanced physiologic collapse may substantially weaken the ability to establish that earlier intervention probably would have prevented the final outcome despite apparent deviation.

Importantly, this distinction does not eliminate the significance of delayed care, operational weakness, or clinical deviation.

A deviation may still carry substantial regulatory, ethical, operational, or professional significance even when sustainable causation remains difficult to establish.

But litigation ultimately requires more than identifying imperfection alone.

It requires establishing that the identified failure probably altered the patient's clinical trajectory beyond what would otherwise have occurred through the underlying disease process itself.

This is one of the central principles of Causation Mapping within the Lexcura Clinical Intelligence Model™: Medicine allows possibility. Litigation requires probability.

The Role Of Baseline Physiologic Reserve In Causation

One of the most important variables within Causation Mapping is the patient's baseline physiologic reserve before the deterioration itself began.

Not all patients enter clinical deterioration with the same capacity for reversibility, recovery, compensation, or survival.

Some patients possess substantial reserve despite acute illness. Others begin the progression already functioning near the limits of physiologic compensation because of advanced chronic disease, frailty, progressive organ dysfunction, severe comorbid burden, malnutrition, metastatic disease, recurrent hospitalization, or prolonged systemic decline.

Causation analysis depends heavily upon whether meaningful recovery opportunity realistically existed during the progression itself.

A patient with strong baseline reserve may tolerate delayed intervention, temporary instability, or progressive deterioration longer before irreversible collapse develops.

Conversely, a severely compromised patient may possess minimal physiologic capacity to withstand even relatively short periods of worsening instability despite otherwise appropriate intervention efforts.

For this reason, Causation Mapping evaluates not only what occurred during the deterioration itself, but the physiologic condition in which the patient entered the progression.

This includes examining baseline organ function, chronic disease burden, prior functional status, frailty, nutritional condition, recurrent admissions, oxygen dependence, cardiovascular reserve, renal function, immune compromise, neurologic baseline, and overall physiologic resilience before the acute event developed.

Importantly, severe baseline illness does not automatically eliminate causation.

A critically vulnerable patient may still possess meaningful intervention opportunity during portions of the progression itself. Earlier escalation, faster intervention, more aggressive treatment, or more timely recognition may still materially alter outcome even in medically fragile individuals when reversibility remains physiologically plausible.

However, baseline vulnerability may substantially weaken the ability to establish that earlier intervention probably would have prevented the final outcome when the patient already possessed profoundly limited reserve before the alleged deviation occurred.

This distinction often becomes one of the central battlegrounds within medical litigation.

Plaintiff analysis may emphasize delayed recognition, narrowing intervention opportunity, or progression worsening during the sequence itself.

Defense analysis may emphasize severe baseline compromise, overwhelming disease burden, progressive decline, limited reversibility, or underlying physiologic instability that substantially weakened survivability regardless of intervention timing.

The strength of causation therefore depends not solely upon identifying delay or deviation, but upon determining whether the patient's underlying physiologic condition realistically allowed meaningful recovery opportunity during the progression itself.

This is why Baseline Profiling and Causation Mapping remain deeply interconnected within the Lexcura Clinical Intelligence Model™.

Because before litigation can determine whether a deviation altered outcome, the analysis must first determine how much physiologic reserve existed before the deterioration ever began.

The Role Of Timing In Causation Analysis

Timing is one of the most critical components of Causation Mapping.

Because in medical litigation, the strength of causation often depends not simply upon whether a deviation occurred, but when the deviation occurred relative to the progression of physiologic deterioration itself.

Deterioration is rarely static.

Clinical instability evolves over time. Intervention opportunity may narrow progressively as shock worsens, organ dysfunction advances, oxygen debt accumulates, neurologic injury progresses, hemorrhage expands, infection disseminates, or irreversible physiologic collapse develops throughout the sequence of care.

For this reason, Causation Mapping evaluates whether meaningful reversibility remained realistically present during the actual delay period itself.

In some matters, deterioration remains highly salvageable during the progression. Earlier escalation, antibiotic administration, operative intervention, airway management, hemorrhage control, cardiac intervention, neurologic decompression, or ICU transfer may substantially alter outcome because physiologic collapse has not yet become irreversible during the sequence itself.

In other matters, deterioration may already be significantly advanced before the alleged deviation occurs.

A patient may present late in the disease process. Severe organ dysfunction may already be established before recognition delays develop. Irreversible ischemia, overwhelming infection, catastrophic neurologic injury, or progressive physiologic collapse may already be evolving despite subsequent intervention opportunity.

Because the same delay may carry profoundly different causation significance depending upon when it occurred relative to the progression of physiologic injury.

A two-hour delay in one patient may possess minimal causation impact if irreversible deterioration had already developed before the delay itself began.

Conversely, a relatively short delay in another patient may become critically important if meaningful reversibility remained highly time-sensitive during that intervention window.

For this reason, Causation Mapping closely evaluates chronology progression alongside physiologic evolution.

The analysis examines when instability first became clinically actionable, when intervention opportunity remained realistically salvageable, when deterioration accelerated, when organ dysfunction became increasingly irreversible, and whether earlier intervention probably would have altered the trajectory before irreversible collapse developed.

Importantly, timing analysis does not evaluate chronology in isolation alone.

The same temporal delay may produce very different physiologic consequences depending upon baseline reserve, disease severity, treatment responsiveness, age, comorbid burden, and progression stability throughout the sequence itself.

This is why Timeline Reconstruction and Causation Mapping remain deeply interconnected within the Lexcura Clinical Intelligence Model™.

Because before litigation can determine whether delay materially altered outcome, the analysis must determine where that delay occurred within the actual physiologic progression of deterioration.

And in many medical negligence cases, causation ultimately depends not merely upon whether intervention was delayed, but whether the delay occurred during a period when meaningful reversibility still realistically existed.

The Difference Between Temporal Association And True Causation

One of the most common analytical errors in medical litigation is confusing temporal association with true causation.

A patient deteriorates after a delay. An intervention occurs late.

A catastrophic outcome follows a visible deviation within the chronology.

At first review, the sequence may appear causally straightforward simply because the adverse outcome occurred after the identified failure.

However, temporal sequence alone does not automatically establish that the deviation caused the outcome.

Critically ill patients often deteriorate through complex underlying disease processes that may continue progressing despite intervention efforts.

A patient may worsen after delayed escalation while simultaneously experiencing overwhelming sepsis, advanced malignancy, catastrophic hemorrhage, severe respiratory failure, irreversible neurologic injury, or progressive multi-organ collapse already capable of producing the final outcome independently.

For this reason, Causation Mapping does not assume that chronology alone establishes causation.

The analysis instead evaluates whether the identified deviation plausibly altered the physiologic trajectory itself beyond what would otherwise have occurred through the underlying disease progression.

In some matters, the temporal relationship strongly supports causation.

A patient may remain relatively stable before a delay period, deteriorate progressively during the absence of intervention, and improve substantially once definitive treatment is finally initiated. In those circumstances, the chronology itself may strongly reinforce the physiologic plausibility of causation.

In other matters, the temporal relationship may appear superficially compelling while deeper physiologic analysis substantially weakens causation support.

A patient may continue deteriorating despite timely intervention. Severe organ dysfunction may already have been established before the alleged deviation occurred.

Progressive collapse may continue despite aggressive treatment because the underlying disease process had already advanced beyond meaningful reversibility.

Because temporal proximity alone is not the same as physiologic causation.

The fact that deterioration followed a deviation does not automatically establish that the deviation materially changed the outcome.

For this reason, Causation Mapping evaluates not only when deterioration occurred, but whether the sequence demonstrates a defensible physiologic relationship between the alleged failure and the progression of injury itself.

This includes examining treatment responsiveness, progression acceleration, reversibility, intervention timing, baseline reserve, competing disease processes, and whether earlier intervention probably would have changed the trajectory in a meaningful way.

Importantly, this distinction does not minimize the significance of delay, deviation, or operational weakness.

A deviation may still represent poor care, regulatory concern, or professional failure even when causation remains physiologically uncertain.

But litigation ultimately requires more than temporal association alone.

It requires evidence supporting that the identified failure probably altered the clinical progression beyond what would otherwise have occurred through the underlying disease process itself.

This is one of the central principles of Causation Mapping within the Lexcura Clinical Intelligence Model™: Chronology may suggest causation. Physiology must support it.

The Danger Of Retrospective Outcome Bias

One of the greatest challenges within Causation Mapping is avoiding retrospective outcome bias during litigation analysis.

Once a catastrophic outcome occurs, the chronology often appears far more predictable in hindsight than it realistically appeared during the actual progression of care.

Reviewers evaluate the sequence while already knowing the final outcome. The patient died.

The hemorrhage progressed. The sepsis worsened.

The neurologic injury became irreversible. The cardiac arrest occurred.

Because the outcome is already known, there is a natural tendency to reinterpret earlier findings as more obviously dangerous, actionable, or preventable than they may initially have appeared in real time.

Subtle abnormalities that later proved significant may seem unmistakable in retrospect. Delays may appear more unreasonable once the final outcome becomes visible. Early warning signs may appear more predictive after irreversible deterioration has already occurred.

However, causation analysis cannot rely upon hindsight reconstruction alone.

Providers make decisions within evolving clinical conditions filled with uncertainty, competing diagnoses, incomplete information, fluctuating symptoms, and variable physiologic presentation during the actual sequence itself.

For this reason, Causation Mapping evaluates not only what ultimately happened, but what was reasonably recognizable, actionable, and physiologically apparent at the time the decisions were made.

In some matters, the deterioration pattern may truly have been obvious, progressive, and highly actionable before the delay occurred. The chronology may strongly support that earlier recognition and intervention probably would have altered the outcome.

In others, the progression may have been clinically ambiguous, rapidly evolving, atypical, or initially nonspecific despite later catastrophic deterioration.

Medical litigation is inherently retrospective.

Because the fact that a catastrophic outcome ultimately occurred does not automatically establish that providers reasonably should have predicted the full extent of that deterioration earlier in the sequence.

Similarly, the presence of a delay does not automatically establish that earlier intervention probably would have prevented the final outcome.

Retrospective outcome bias may substantially distort both breach analysis and causation analysis when reviewers unconsciously interpret earlier findings through the lens of the known outcome rather than through the uncertainty that existed during the actual progression itself.

For this reason, Causation Mapping requires disciplined physiologic reconstruction rather than hindsight-driven assumption.

The analysis must determine what intervention opportunity realistically existed at the time, how clinically actionable the deterioration appeared during the progression itself, and whether earlier intervention probably would have altered the trajectory before irreversible collapse developed.

This is one of the central principles of Causation Mapping within the Lexcura Clinical Intelligence Model™: A known outcome may reshape perception of the chronology.

But sustainable causation requires analysis grounded in real-time physiologic reality rather than retrospective certainty.

The Role Of Reversibility In Causation Analysis

One of the most important questions within Causation Mapping is whether the patient's deterioration remained meaningfully reversible during the period in which the alleged deviation occurred.

Causation depends not only upon identifying delay, deviation, or operational failure, but upon determining whether intervention opportunity still realistically existed before irreversible physiologic collapse developed.

Not all deterioration remains reversible throughout the progression of care.

Some disease processes retain substantial salvageability even during significant instability. Others progress rapidly toward irreversible organ failure, neurologic injury, circulatory collapse, overwhelming infection, or catastrophic physiologic exhaustion despite aggressive intervention efforts.

For this reason, Causation Mapping evaluates whether meaningful recovery opportunity remained physiologically plausible during the actual delay period itself. In some matters, reversibility remains strong.

A septic patient may still respond favorably to earlier antibiotic administration, fluid resuscitation, vasopressor support, or ICU escalation before profound shock and multi-organ failure fully develop. A stroke patient may retain meaningful neurologic salvageability before ischemic injury becomes irreversible. A hemorrhaging patient may remain recoverable before prolonged hypoperfusion produces catastrophic physiologic collapse.

In these circumstances, relatively short delays may materially alter outcome because the deterioration remained highly time-sensitive and physiologically reversible during the progression itself.

In other matters, reversibility may already be substantially limited before the alleged deviation occurs.

A patient may present with overwhelming sepsis, prolonged untreated ischemia, advanced respiratory failure, devastating traumatic injury, severe multi-organ dysfunction, or progressive terminal disease already approaching irreversible collapse despite subsequent intervention efforts.

In those situations, the ability to establish that earlier intervention probably would have changed the final outcome may weaken substantially even when portions of care appear operationally deficient.

Temporal proximity alone is not the same as physiologic causation.

Because the presence of delay alone does not establish that the outcome remained preventable during the progression itself.

The analysis must determine whether meaningful physiologic salvageability still realistically existed at the time intervention opportunity allegedly narrowed.

Importantly, reversibility is rarely absolute.

Patients may partially improve despite severe deterioration. Certain injuries may become irreversible while other aspects of decline remain potentially modifiable.

Some interventions may prolong survival without preventing the ultimate outcome entirely.

For this reason, Causation Mapping evaluates not only whether complete recovery remained possible, but whether earlier intervention probably would have materially altered the clinical trajectory in a meaningful way.

This includes examining treatment responsiveness, progression stability, organ dysfunction severity, intervention timing, baseline reserve, disease burden, and the physiologic window in which meaningful recovery opportunity remained realistically present.

This is why reversibility serves as one of the central physiologic anchors within the Lexcura Clinical Intelligence Model™.

Because before litigation can establish sustainable causation, the analysis must determine whether the patient's deterioration remained meaningfully reversible during the actual progression of care.

The *Difference Between Contributing Factors And Primary Causation*

One of the most difficult aspects of Causation Mapping is determining whether an identified deviation merely contributed to the progression of deterioration or whether it served as a primary causal factor materially altering the final outcome.

This distinction matters because complex medical deterioration rarely develops through one isolated variable alone.

Critically ill patients often deteriorate through multiple interacting physiologic, operational, and disease-related processes occurring simultaneously throughout the sequence of care.

A patient may experience delayed escalation while also suffering overwhelming infection. A reassessment delay may occur during progressive multi-organ dysfunction already associated with high mortality risk. Communication failures may coexist alongside advanced frailty, severe baseline illness, delayed presentation, catastrophic injury burden, or rapidly evolving physiologic collapse.

For this reason, Causation Mapping does not evaluate deviations in isolation alone.

The analysis instead examines the relative influence of the identified failure within the broader progression of deterioration itself.

In some matters, the deviation appears central to the outcome progression.

A delayed intervention may directly impair hemorrhage control, postpone sepsis treatment, delay operative management, prolong hypoxia, or significantly narrow intervention opportunity during a period when meaningful reversibility remained highly plausible.

In those circumstances, the deviation may function as a primary causal driver materially influencing the patient's clinical trajectory.

In other matters, the identified deviation may function more as a secondary contributing factor within an already overwhelming disease process.

A patient may already possess severe irreversible organ dysfunction, advanced physiologic exhaustion, catastrophic neurologic injury, or progressive terminal decline before the alleged deviation occurs. Although the operational failure may still represent poor care or regulatory concern, the underlying disease burden itself may remain the dominant driver of the final outcome.

Contributing influence alone is not always sufficient to establish strong sustainable causation.

The analysis must determine whether the identified failure materially altered the progression itself beyond what would otherwise have occurred through the underlying physiologic process.

Importantly, contributing factors may still carry substantial legal and strategic significance.

A deviation may worsen suffering, accelerate deterioration, narrow recovery opportunity, prolong instability, increase procedural burden, or contribute meaningfully to portions of the injury sequence even when it does not independently function as the dominant cause of death or catastrophic decline.

For this reason, Causation Mapping evaluates both the existence and the relative weight of each contributing factor within the progression itself.

This includes examining disease severity, timing, baseline reserve, intervention responsiveness, competing physiologic processes, progression stability, and whether the identified deviation materially changed the trajectory in a meaningful and defensible way.

This is one of the central principles of Causation Mapping within the Lexcura Clinical Intelligence Model™: Not every contributing factor functions as primary causation.

The analysis must determine how much influence the identified failure actually exerted upon the progression of deterioration itself.

The Role Of Competing Physiologic Processes

One of the most complex aspects of Causation Mapping is evaluating how competing physiologic processes influence outcome progression during medical deterioration.

Critically ill patients rarely deteriorate through one isolated mechanism alone.

Multiple disease processes frequently evolve simultaneously throughout the sequence of care, interacting in ways that may substantially complicate causation analysis.

A septic patient may also possess advanced cardiac disease, chronic renal failure, respiratory compromise, severe malnutrition, and progressive immune dysfunction.

A trauma patient may simultaneously experience hemorrhage, hypoxia, inflammatory response, neurologic injury, and metabolic collapse. A postoperative patient may deteriorate through overlapping infection, circulatory instability, organ dysfunction, and progressive physiologic exhaustion occurring at the same time.

In some matters, one dominant process clearly drives the progression.

A rapidly expanding hemorrhage, untreated airway compromise, evolving septic shock, or delayed operative emergency may remain the primary physiologic force shaping the outcome trajectory despite the presence of secondary comorbid conditions.

In other matters, multiple competing processes may simultaneously contribute to worsening instability, making it substantially more difficult to determine whether one individual deviation materially altered the final outcome.

A patient may continue deteriorating despite intervention because severe baseline illness, advanced organ dysfunction, progressive inflammatory injury, or overwhelming disease burden independently limit survivability regardless of escalation timing.

For this reason, Causation Mapping evaluates how competing physiologic mechanisms interacted throughout the progression itself rather than assuming one isolated failure fully explains the outcome.

The analysis examines whether the identified deviation realistically altered the dominant physiologic trajectory or whether the underlying disease processes themselves remained sufficiently overwhelming to produce the outcome independently.

Complex deterioration can create the illusion of strong causation through timing alone while the underlying physiology remains substantially more multifactorial.

Importantly, the presence of competing physiologic processes does not automatically eliminate causation.

A deviation may still materially worsen instability, accelerate deterioration, narrow intervention opportunity, or contribute meaningfully to the progression even in medically complex patients with severe underlying disease burden.

However, sustainable causation requires demonstrating that the identified failure exerted meaningful physiologic influence within the broader progression itself rather than merely existing alongside independent deterioration processes already capable of producing the final outcome.

For this reason, Causation Mapping requires layered physiologic reconstruction rather than simplified retrospective association.

This is one of the central principles of the Lexcura Clinical Intelligence Model™:
Medical deterioration often progresses through multiple interacting physiologic mechanisms simultaneously.

Causation analysis must determine which processes actually drove the progression of injury during the sequence of care.

The Role Of Treatment Responsiveness In Causation Analysis

One of the most important indicators within Causation Mapping is how the patient responded physiologically to intervention during the progression of care.

Treatment responsiveness may provide critical insight into whether meaningful reversibility remained present during the deterioration itself.

Causation analysis does not evaluate delay alone.

It evaluates whether the patient's physiology still retained the capacity to improve once intervention occurred.

In some matters, treatment responsiveness strongly supports causation.

A patient may deteriorate progressively during a delay period, then improve substantially once antibiotics, airway management, operative intervention, hemorrhage control, vasopressor support, decompression, or critical care escalation is finally initiated.

Blood pressure stabilizes. Lactate improves.

Oxygenation recovers. Mental status normalizes.

Organ dysfunction begins reversing.

In these circumstances, the physiologic response itself may strongly support the conclusion that earlier intervention probably would have altered the progression in a meaningful way.

The chronology and physiology begin reinforcing one another.

In other matters, treatment responsiveness may remain minimal despite aggressive intervention efforts.

A patient may continue deteriorating despite timely antibiotics, ICU transfer, operative management, ventilatory support, vasopressor escalation, or aggressive resuscitation. Progressive organ failure may continue worsening despite appropriate intervention because the underlying disease process had already advanced beyond meaningful reversibility before the delay itself became clinically significant.

Because poor treatment responsiveness may substantially weaken the argument that earlier intervention probably would have prevented the final outcome.

Conversely, strong physiologic recovery following delayed intervention may strengthen the argument that meaningful salvageability remained present during the progression itself.

For this reason, Causation Mapping evaluates not only when intervention occurred, but how the patient physiologically responded once intervention was initiated.

The analysis examines stabilization patterns, organ recovery, treatment effectiveness, progression slowing, hemodynamic response, neurologic improvement, respiratory recovery, infection control, and whether intervention produced meaningful physiologic improvement during the sequence itself.

Importantly, treatment responsiveness is rarely absolute.

Some patients demonstrate partial recovery while still experiencing catastrophic outcome. Others may initially stabilize before progressive deterioration later resumes. Certain organ systems may improve while others continue failing despite aggressive intervention efforts.

For this reason, treatment responsiveness must be interpreted within the broader physiologic context surrounding the progression itself.

This includes evaluating baseline reserve, disease severity, timing of intervention, competing physiologic processes, progression stability, and whether the observed response realistically supports sustainable causation under scrutiny.

This is one of the central principles of Causation Mapping within the Lexcura Clinical Intelligence Model™: The patient's physiologic response to intervention may provide critical insight into whether meaningful reversibility still existed during the progression of deterioration.

CASE ANALYSIS - 1

Delayed Sepsis Recognition With Strong Causation Support

A 54-year-old female presented to the emergency department with fever, tachycardia, hypotension, elevated white blood cell count, worsening confusion, elevated lactate, and findings concerning for progressive sepsis secondary to pneumonia.

Initial nursing documentation reflected repeated episodes of worsening instability over several hours. Blood pressure continued declining, oxygen requirements progressively increased, urine output diminished, and mental status became increasingly altered throughout the progression.

Despite these findings, physician reassessment remained delayed. Broad-spectrum antibiotics were not initiated promptly, ICU escalation did not occur until significantly later in the sequence, and vasopressor support was delayed despite progressive hypotension and worsening signs of septic shock.

At intake, the chronology appeared highly concerning.

The patient deteriorated steadily during a prolonged period in which actionable instability remained visible within the record.

However, deeper Causation Mapping analysis became critically important in determining whether the delays merely occurred alongside the deterioration or whether they materially altered the patient's final outcome.

Importantly, the patient possessed relatively strong baseline physiologic reserve before the event developed.

The records demonstrated no advanced organ failure, no severe baseline frailty, no terminal disease process, and no major preexisting physiologic instability substantially limiting reversibility before the sepsis progression began.

The chronology also demonstrated that portions of the deterioration remained responsive once definitive intervention was finally initiated.

After ICU transfer, aggressive fluid resuscitation, vasopressor support, ventilatory management, and delayed antibiotic administration, portions of the patient's hemodynamic instability initially improved. Lactate levels temporarily stabilized, blood pressure partially recovered, and oxygenation improved for a period following escalation of care.

The physiology itself suggested that meaningful reversibility likely remained present during portions of the delay period.

As the analysis deepened, the causation framework became increasingly strong.

The patient's instability progressed steadily during a period in which earlier sepsis recognition, antibiotic administration, vasopressor initiation, and ICU escalation likely remained highly time-sensitive and physiologically actionable.

Unlike cases involving overwhelming irreversible collapse before the deviation occurred, this chronology demonstrated a progression in which intervention opportunity appeared meaningfully salvageable during the actual delay itself.

The litigation analysis therefore shifted beyond merely identifying delayed care.

The deeper conclusion became that the delays probably altered the patient's physiologic trajectory during a period when meaningful reversibility still realistically existed.

Importantly, this did not require proving absolute certainty that earlier intervention would have guaranteed survival.

Medicine rarely permits that level of certainty.

However, the chronology, treatment responsiveness, baseline reserve, and progression pattern collectively supported the conclusion that earlier intervention more likely than not would have materially improved the patient's outcome.

This is one of the central principles of Causation Mapping within the Lexcura Clinical Intelligence Model™: Strong causation often emerges when delayed intervention occurs during a period in which meaningful physiologic reversibility still realistically existed.

CASE ANALYSIS - 2

Severe Baseline Compromise With Weakened Causation Support

An 81-year-old male with advanced congestive heart failure, severe chronic kidney disease, insulin-dependent diabetes, chronic obstructive pulmonary disease, recurrent hospitalization history, and significant baseline frailty presented to the emergency department with worsening shortness of breath, hypotension, confusion, metabolic acidosis, and progressive respiratory distress.

Initial review of the chronology revealed several concerning delays.

Reassessment intervals became inconsistent during portions of the progression. ICU transfer occurred later than expected, physician escalation appeared fragmented, and portions of the respiratory deterioration progressed before definitive ventilatory intervention was initiated.

At intake, the case appeared strongly supportive of causation.

The patient deteriorated progressively during a visible period of delayed escalation, and the family strongly believed earlier intervention would have prevented the patient's death.

However, deeper Causation Mapping analysis substantially complicated the litigation framework.

The patient entered the progression with profoundly limited physiologic reserve before the deterioration itself began.

The records demonstrated severe baseline cardiac dysfunction, chronic oxygen dependence, recurrent decompensation episodes, advanced renal impairment, poor functional status, and evidence of progressive multi-system decline preceding the acute event.

Importantly, portions of the deterioration also appeared significantly advanced before the alleged delays became clinically actionable.

Laboratory findings already demonstrated severe metabolic instability, worsening renal failure, escalating inflammatory burden, and progressive respiratory compromise early in the sequence itself.

As the analysis progressed, treatment responsiveness remained limited despite aggressive intervention efforts.

Following ICU transfer, vasopressor support, ventilatory management, broad spectrum antibiotics, and critical care escalation, the patient continued demonstrating progressive multi-organ dysfunction with minimal sustained physiologic recovery. Hypotension persisted.

Renal failure worsened.

Respiratory collapse progressed despite escalating support.

The physiology itself suggested that meaningful reversibility may already have been substantially limited before portions of the delay period occurred.

As a result, the litigation analysis shifted away from whether delays simply existed and toward whether those delays probably altered the final outcome in a meaningful and defensible way.

The operational concerns remained important.

The chronology still supported criticism regarding escalation timing, reassessment continuity, and portions of the response sequence.

However, the deeper causation analysis became substantially weaker because the underlying physiologic trajectory itself appeared overwhelmingly severe even before the alleged deviations developed.

This distinction materially altered the litigation posture.

Because although earlier intervention may theoretically have improved portions of the progression, the available physiology provided significantly less support for the conclusion that earlier intervention probably would have prevented the final outcome.

This is one of the central principles of Causation Mapping within the Lexcura Clinical Intelligence Model™: The presence of delay alone does not establish strong causation.

The analysis must determine whether meaningful physiologic reversibility still realistically existed during the progression itself.

Applying Causation Mapping

Understanding Causation Mapping conceptually is only the beginning. The true importance of this pillar becomes apparent when physiologic progression, intervention timing, baseline reserve, and reversibility are evaluated within actual litigation reconstruction.

In practice, Causation Mapping determines whether the identified deviation materially altered the patient's physiologic trajectory during a period when meaningful recovery opportunity still realistically existed.

The analysis evaluates far more than whether deterioration occurred.

It examines how baseline reserve, progression timing, treatment responsiveness, competing physiologic processes, intervention opportunity, and reversibility interacted throughout the actual sequence of care.

The following exercise is designed to apply these principles within a realistic medical litigation setting.

As you review the chronology, it is important to evaluate not only whether delays occurred, but whether those delays probably altered the patient's outcome in a meaningful and physiologically defensible way.

Consider whether meaningful reversibility remained present during the progression itself. Evaluate how baseline reserve influenced survivability, whether intervention opportunity narrowed during the sequence, whether competing physiologic processes independently threatened the outcome, and whether the patient demonstrated evidence of treatment responsiveness once escalation ultimately occurred.

This distinction forms one of the central analytical foundations of the Lexcura Clinical Intelligence Model™.

Because causation analysis depends not merely upon identifying delay or deviation, but upon determining whether the identified failure probably changed the physiologic trajectory during the actual progression of deterioration.

Evaluating Reversibility During Progressive Septic Deterioration

A 63-year-old male presented to the emergency department with fever, tachycardia, worsening confusion, elevated lactate, hypotension, leukocytosis, and respiratory findings concerning for evolving sepsis secondary to pneumonia.

Initial nursing documentation reflected progressive instability throughout several hours following presentation. Blood pressure gradually declined, oxygen requirements increased, urine output diminished, and mental status became increasingly altered during the progression itself.

Despite these findings, physician reassessment remained delayed during portions of the sequence. Broad-spectrum antibiotics were not initiated promptly, ICU escalation occurred significantly later in the chronology, and vasopressor support was delayed despite worsening hypotension and progressive septic instability.

The patient eventually required ICU transfer, mechanical ventilation, vasopressor support, and aggressive critical care intervention following progression into septic shock.

Importantly, the patient possessed moderate baseline chronic illness before the event developed, including hypertension, controlled diabetes, and mild chronic kidney disease. However, the records demonstrated no advanced organ failure, no severe baseline frailty, no terminal disease process, and no evidence of profound physiologic collapse before the deterioration itself began.

Following ICU transfer and escalation of care, portions of the patient's physiology initially responded to intervention. Blood pressure temporarily improved with vasopressor support, oxygenation partially stabilized following ventilatory management, and portions of the metabolic abnormalities demonstrated transient improvement before subsequent deterioration later resumed.

The patient ultimately died five days later following progressive multi-organ failure complications related to septic shock.

As part of the Lexcura Clinical Intelligence Model™, your task is to evaluate whether the identified delays probably altered the patient's physiologic trajectory during a period in which meaningful reversibility still realistically existed.

Questions For Analysis

As you evaluate this case, consider not only whether delays occurred, but whether the identified delays probably altered the patient's physiologic trajectory during the progression itself.

At what point did the patient's deterioration become sufficiently actionable to require more aggressive intervention, ICU escalation, vasopressor initiation, or physician reassessment? Consider how the worsening hypotension, escalating oxygen requirements, declining urine output, worsening confusion, and progressive septic instability influenced intervention urgency as the chronology evolved.

How did the patient's baseline physiologic reserve affect causation analysis? Did the absence of advanced frailty, terminal illness, severe organ failure, or profound baseline physiologic compromise strengthen the argument that meaningful reversibility remained present during portions of the delay period?

To what extent did timing influence the progression itself? Consider whether earlier antibiotic administration, faster escalation, earlier vasopressor support, or more timely ICU transfer probably would have altered the patient's physiologic trajectory before septic shock and progressive multi-organ dysfunction became increasingly established.

How should the patient's initial treatment responsiveness influence the analysis?

Do the temporary improvements in blood pressure, oxygenation, and metabolic stability following ICU escalation suggest that meaningful physiologic salvageability still existed during portions of the progression itself?

What competing physiologic processes were present during the deterioration? Did the patient's moderate chronic illness independently create overwhelming irreversible collapse, or did the chronology primarily support progressive septic deterioration occurring during a potentially salvageable intervention window?

Most importantly, based upon the progression itself, does the available physiology support the conclusion that the identified delays probably altered the patient's outcome in a meaningful and defensible way, or does the evidence support only theoretical possibility rather than sustainable causation?

Answer Key & Analysis

The central analytical issue in this case is not simply whether delays occurred during the patient's septic deterioration.

The deeper issue is whether those delays probably altered the patient's physiologic trajectory during a period in which meaningful reversibility still realistically existed. At first review, the chronology appears strongly supportive of causation.

The patient demonstrated progressive hypotension, worsening oxygen requirements, declining urine output, escalating confusion, and increasing septic instability over several hours before definitive escalation ultimately occurred. Antibiotic administration was delayed, ICU transfer occurred later in the progression, and vasopressor support was not initiated promptly despite worsening shock physiology.

An attorney initially reviewing the sequence may reasonably conclude that the delays substantially contributed to the patient's eventual death.

However, deeper Causation Mapping analysis requires evaluating not only whether delays occurred, but whether the patient's physiology remained meaningfully salvageable during the progression itself.

Importantly, the patient possessed moderate - but not profoundly limiting - baseline illness before the deterioration began.

The records demonstrated hypertension, controlled diabetes, and mild chronic kidney disease, yet there was no evidence of advanced frailty, terminal disease, severe baseline organ failure, or catastrophic preexisting physiologic instability substantially limiting reversibility before the septic progression developed.

This distinction becomes highly significant.

Because the patient entered the deterioration with substantially greater physiologic reserve than many medically catastrophic causation cases.

The chronology also demonstrated evidence of treatment responsiveness once definitive intervention finally occurred.

Following ICU transfer, vasopressor support, ventilatory management, and aggressive critical care escalation, portions of the patient's physiology initially improved. Blood pressure partially stabilized, oxygenation improved temporarily, and metabolic abnormalities demonstrated transient recovery before subsequent deterioration later resumed.

This treatment responsiveness materially strengthens causation analysis.

Because the physiology itself suggests that meaningful reversibility likely remained present during portions of the delay period.

The patient did not demonstrate immediate irreversible collapse despite escalation.

Instead, the chronology supports a progression in which portions of the septic instability initially remained physiologically responsive once definitive intervention was finally initiated.

The case no longer involves merely identifying delayed care.

The deeper conclusion becomes that the identified delays likely occurred during a period in which earlier intervention probably would have altered the physiologic trajectory in a meaningful way.

Importantly, this does not require proving with absolute certainty that earlier intervention would have guaranteed survival.

Medicine rarely permits that level of certainty.

However, sustainable causation does not require absolute certainty.

It requires demonstrating that earlier recognition, escalation, antibiotic administration, vasopressor initiation, and ICU transfer more likely than not would have materially improved the patient's progression before septic shock and irreversible multi-organ dysfunction became fully established.

The chronology, baseline reserve, intervention timing, and treatment responsiveness collectively support that conclusion.

This is one of the central principles of Causation Mapping within the Lexcura Clinical Intelligence Model™: Strong causation often emerges when delayed intervention occurs during a progression in which meaningful physiologic reversibility still realistically existed.

Chapter 6 Takeaways

Causation Mapping

1. Causation requires more than a bad outcome.

The analysis must determine whether the identified failure probably altered the patient's physiologic trajectory during the actual progression of care.

2. Medicine allows possibility. Litigation requires probability.

Sustainable causation requires evidence that the identified failure more likely than not materially altered the outcome in a meaningful and physiologically defensible way.

3. Baseline physiologic reserve strongly influences causation strength.

Severe frailty, advanced chronic illness, and limited reserve may substantially weaken reversibility despite delayed intervention.

4. Timing defines causation significance.

The same delay may carry profoundly different meaning depending upon where it occurred within the progression of deterioration.

5. Temporal association alone does not establish causation.

Chronology may suggest causation, but the physiology must support it.

6. Retrospective outcome bias may distort analysis.

Sustainable causation requires real-time physiologic reconstruction rather than hindsight-driven assumption.

7. Reversibility remains central to causation analysis.

The analysis must determine whether meaningful physiologic salvageability still realistically existed during the progression itself.

8. Not every contributing factor functions as primary causation.

Complex deterioration often develops through multiple interacting physiologic and operational processes simultaneously.

9. Competing physiologic processes may weaken or complicate causation.

The analysis must determine which mechanisms actually drove the progression of injury during the sequence of care.

10. Treatment responsiveness may significantly influence causation strength.

Physiologic improvement following delayed intervention may support the conclusion that meaningful reversibility still remained present.

11. Causation Mapping requires layered physiologic reconstruction.

Timing, reversibility, baseline reserve, treatment responsiveness, competing disease processes, and progression stability must be evaluated together rather than in isolation.

12. Sustainable causation depends upon physiologic plausibility.

Before litigation can responsibly attribute liability, the analysis must determine whether the identified failure probably altered the patient's physiologic trajectory during a period in which meaningful reversibility still realistically existed.

Transition To The Next Pillar

Once Causation Mapping determines whether an identified failure probably altered the patient's physiologic trajectory, the analysis reaches a final and equally critical stage: How should those findings ultimately be translated into litigation strategy?

This is where Litigation-Ready Output becomes essential within the Lexcura Clinical Intelligence Model™.

Because even the strongest clinical analysis may lose substantial value if it cannot be communicated clearly, organized strategically, defended under scrutiny, and translated into a structure attorneys can actually use in active litigation.

Medical litigation does not depend solely upon identifying clinical truth.

It depends upon the ability to construct a clear, physiologically coherent, evidentiary supported explanation of how the progression unfolded, why the deterioration mattered, how the operational failures influenced the sequence, and whether the conclusions remain sustainable under adversarial review.

A chronology may contain important findings, yet still become ineffective if the analysis appears speculative, emotionally driven, disorganized, inconsistent, excessively technical, or poorly connected to the actual physiologic progression of care.

Similarly, even accurate conclusions may weaken substantially if the reasoning pathway linking chronology reconstruction, baseline profiling, standard-of-care analysis, regulatory evaluation, and causation remains unclear or structurally fragmented.

For this reason, Litigation-Ready Output serves as the final integration pillar within the Lexcura Clinical Intelligence Model™.

This pillar transforms complex clinical analysis into organized litigation intelligence capable of supporting attorneys, experts, mediators, insurers, judges, and juries throughout the adversarial process itself.

The analysis must ultimately withstand expert scrutiny, deposition challenge, evidentiary review, defense criticism, and physiologic cross-examination while remaining internally consistent, strategically coherent, and medically defensible from beginning to end.

Medical litigation is not won merely through identifying deviation.

It is won through the ability to explain - clearly, logically, and defensibly - how the clinical progression unfolded and why the conclusions remain sustainable under scrutiny.

The final pillar therefore examines how complex medical findings are converted into litigation-grade clinical intelligence capable of supporting real-world legal strategy.

Because before medical analysis can influence legal outcome, the findings themselves must become operationally organized, strategically usable, and defensibly structured for the realities of litigation practice.

CHAPTER - 07

LITIGATION READY OUTPUT

Transforming clinical analysis into strategic litigation intelligence.

This chapter establishes a foundational pillar within the Lexcura Clinical Intelligence Model™ creating the evidentiary framework required for defensible medical-legal analysis.

STRUCTURING MEDICAL ANALYSIS FOR LITIGATION READINESS

At intake, the chronology appeared disorganized.

The records contained thousands of pages spread across multiple admissions, nursing notes, physician documentation, laboratory trends, operative reports, medication administration records, consultant evaluations, and fragmented reassessment entries occurring over several weeks of care.

The attorney believed the case involved delayed recognition of progressive postoperative deterioration. Yet despite the volume of information, the progression itself remained difficult to understand.

Critical events were buried throughout the record. Important physiologic changes were separated across disconnected documentation systems. Escalation timing remained unclear. Potential causation concerns existed, but the reasoning pathway connecting deterioration, chronology, operational failures, and outcome progression remained fragmented.

At first review, the problem was not the absence of information. The problem was the absence of structure.

That distinction forms the foundation of Litigation-Ready Output within the Lexcura Clinical Intelligence Model™.

Because in medical litigation, identifying important findings is only part of the process. The analysis must also remain organized, coherent, and strategically usable within litigation.

A case may contain significant clinical failures yet still become strategically weak if the reasoning appears speculative, internally inconsistent, physiologically unsupported, or disconnected from the actual progression of care.

Likewise, even accurate conclusions may lose value if the reasoning supporting those conclusions cannot be followed clearly.

Litigation-Ready Output serves as the final integration pillar within the Lexcura Clinical Intelligence Model™.

This pillar transforms chronology reconstruction, baseline profiling, standard-of-care analysis, regulatory evaluation, and causation mapping into structured litigation intelligence capable of supporting real-world legal strategy.

The purpose of this pillar is not simply to summarize medical records.

It is to construct a coherent analytical framework capable of explaining how the progression unfolded, why the deterioration mattered, where operational or clinical failures emerged, how those failures influenced the trajectory, and why the conclusions remain physiologically sustainable.

Litigation-Ready Output therefore requires far more than clinical accuracy alone.

The analysis must remain logically organized, strategically coherent, physiologically grounded, document-supported, internally consistent, and capable of holding together under challenge.

Medical litigation does not operate like retrospective clinical discussion.

Every conclusion may eventually face cross-examination, expert disagreement, chronology challenge, or competing interpretation regarding the reasoning itself.

Litigation-Ready Output evaluates not only whether the conclusions are clinically correct, but whether the analytical structure remains operationally usable within the realities of litigation practice.

Because before clinical findings can influence legal outcome, the analysis itself must become structured litigation intelligence capable of supporting sustainable legal strategy.

Defining Litigation-Ready Output

Within the Lexcura Clinical Intelligence Model™, Litigation-Ready Output refers to the structured transformation of complex medical analysis into organized, structured, and strategically usable litigation intelligence.

The purpose of this pillar is not simply to present medical findings.

It is to construct a coherent analytical framework capable of sustaining challenge while clearly explaining how the clinical progression unfolded, how the identified failures influenced the trajectory of care, and why the conclusions remain medically and physiologically sustainable under challenge.

Medical records alone do not create litigation strength.

Healthcare documentation is often fragmented, inconsistent, repetitive, poorly sequenced, emotionally reactive, operationally incomplete, or disconnected from the actual progression of deterioration occurring during the sequence of care.

Important findings may exist throughout the record without forming a usable litigation narrative.

Critical escalation failures may appear buried inside hundreds of pages of charting.

Physiologic deterioration may become obscured across disconnected reassessment entries. Operational breakdowns may exist without clear explanation regarding how they influenced the progression itself.

Litigation-Ready Output does not function as simple summarization.

The analysis must organize chronology, physiology, operational failures, standard of care findings, regulatory concerns, and causation conclusions into a structure that remains clear, internally consistent, and strategically sound from beginning to end.

In practice, this requires constructing a reasoning pathway that attorneys, experts, insurers, judges, mediators, and juries can follow logically without becoming lost inside the complexity of the underlying medicine.

The analysis must demonstrate not only what happened, but why the progression mattered, how the deterioration evolved, where intervention opportunities narrowed, how identified failures influenced the trajectory, and whether the conclusions remain sustainable under fact-based and physiologic assessment.

Litigation-Ready Output does not rely upon emotional amplification, speculative language, or hindsight-driven accusation.

The strength of the analysis comes from disciplined chronology reconstruction, physiologic coherence, clear documentary support, internal consistency, and the ability to explain complex medical progression in a manner that remains internally consistent under challenge.

This distinction becomes critically important because medical litigation is inherently adversarial.

Every conclusion may eventually face defense reinterpretation, deposition scrutiny, competing expert analysis, opposition challenge, and direct attack upon the reasoning structure supporting the opinions themselves.

An analysis that appears clinically persuasive at intake may weaken substantially if the chronology becomes inconsistent, the causation framework becomes speculative, the reasoning pathway becomes fragmented, or the conclusions extend beyond what the available physiology can reasonably support.

Litigation-Ready Output evaluates not only whether the medical analysis is accurate, but whether the analytical structure itself remains strategically usable within the realities of litigation practice.

Because before clinical findings can influence legal outcome, the analysis must first become organized litigation intelligence capable of surviving challenge.

The Difference Between Clinical Review And Litigation Analysis

One of the most important distinctions within Litigation-Ready Output is understanding that clinical review and litigation analysis are not the same process. Healthcare providers often review cases from a treatment perspective.

Hospitals may evaluate whether documentation was completed appropriately, whether policies were followed, whether reassessments occurred, or whether providers generally responded within accepted clinical expectations.

While those questions remain important, litigation analysis requires a far more structured and disciplined form of evaluation.

The issue is not simply whether care appears concerning in hindsight.

The issue is whether the chronology, physiology, operational conditions, standard-of care findings, regulatory considerations, and causation framework can be organized into a coherent analytical structure capable of surviving adversarial scrutiny.

Many clinically concerning cases remain weak litigation cases.

A progression may contain delayed reassessment, fragmented documentation, communication breakdown, operational strain, or questionable decision-making while still lacking sustainable causation, clear chronology support, or sufficient physiologic linkage between the identified failures and the ultimate outcome.

Conversely, some of the strongest litigation matters initially appear subtle at intake.

The records may not contain dramatic language or obvious catastrophic events.

However, disciplined chronology reconstruction may reveal progressive deterioration, narrowing intervention opportunity, escalating instability, delayed recognition, operational failure, and physiologically significant intervention windows that substantially strengthen the litigation framework once the progression is analyzed systematically.

Litigation-Ready Output requires more than identifying whether care was "good" or "bad."

The analysis must determine whether the available evidence supports a clear, coherent explanation of how the progression unfolded and whether the identified failures materially influenced the trajectory in a manner capable of surviving scrutiny.

Litigation analysis also differs from ordinary medical review because every conclusion must remain evidentiary anchored.

Assumptions cannot replace documentation. Speculation cannot replace physiology.

Retrospective frustration cannot replace structured reasoning. Conclusions must remain connected to identifiable chronology findings, clinical progression, operational evidence, treatment timing, and physiologic plausibility throughout the analysis itself.

This becomes especially important during deposition and expert challenge.

A clinically persuasive opinion may weaken rapidly if the reasoning pathway becomes inconsistent, unsupported, emotionally overstated, or disconnected from the actual progression documented within the record.

Litigation-Ready Output emphasizes analytical discipline as much as clinical interpretation.

The strength of the analysis comes not from dramatic language or aggressive criticism, but from the ability to construct a coherent analytical framework that remains medically stable under adversarial examination.

Because in medical litigation, conclusions alone are never enough.

The reasoning structure supporting those conclusions must also survive scrutiny.

The Importance Of Analytical Structure

One of the most overlooked weaknesses in medical litigation is the absence of clear analytical structure.

Cases frequently contain important clinical findings, yet the analysis itself becomes difficult to follow because the reasoning pathway is fragmented, inconsistent, overly technical, emotionally reactive, or poorly organized.

Important chronology events may appear disconnected from one another. Physiologic deterioration may be described without clear explanation regarding why it mattered clinically. Operational failures may be identified without demonstrating how those failures influenced the progression itself. Causation opinions may appear conclusory rather than analytically constructed.

As a result, even potentially strong cases may weaken substantially when the analysis lacks organizational clarity.

This distinction becomes critically important because litigation analysis must ultimately communicate complex medical progression to individuals functioning outside the clinical environment itself.

Attorneys, mediators, insurers, judges, and juries may possess varying levels of medical understanding. If the chronology becomes difficult to follow or the reasoning pathway appears inconsistent, the strength of the underlying clinical findings may become significantly diluted during litigation presentation.

Litigation-Ready Output requires disciplined analytical organization from beginning to end. The analysis must move logically through the progression itself.

The chronology must establish how deterioration evolved over time. Baseline profiling must explain the patient's physiologic condition before instability developed. Standard-of-care analysis must identify where intervention expectations emerged within the sequence.

Regulatory analysis must explain how operational systems influenced the progression. Causation analysis must demonstrate whether the identified failures probably altered the trajectory during a period when meaningful reversibility still realistically existed.

Each analytical layer must connect clearly to the next. Structure does not mean oversimplification.

Complex medicine often requires nuanced explanation, competing physiologic interpretation, and layered operational analysis. However, even highly complex cases must remain logically organized if the conclusions are expected to survive adversarial scrutiny.

This becomes especially important during deposition, expert review, and cross examination.

An expert may challenge chronology interpretation. Defense counsel may isolate portions of the progression outside their broader physiologic context. Opposing analysis may attempt to fragment causation reasoning or separate operational failures from the deterioration sequence itself.

Without clear analytical structure, otherwise persuasive conclusions may become increasingly vulnerable under challenge.

Litigation-Ready Output emphasizes organizational discipline as a core component of analytically sound litigation analysis.

Because in medical litigation, the strength of the conclusion often depends upon the clarity and stability of the reasoning structure supporting it.

The Role Of Clarity In Litigation Communication

One of the most important objectives within Litigation-Ready Output is clarity.

Medical litigation frequently involves highly complex physiology, fragmented chronology progression, competing expert interpretation, operational failures, evolving deterioration, and extensive documentation spread across thousands of pages of records.

Yet even the strongest clinical analysis may lose substantial value if the reasoning becomes difficult to follow.

Litigation ultimately depends upon communication as much as analysis itself.

An attorney may understand the medicine only partially. A mediator may focus primarily upon risk exposure. A judge may possess no clinical background whatsoever.

A jury may encounter complex medical terminology for the first time during trial presentation.

If the analytical structure becomes excessively technical, poorly organized, inconsistent, or unnecessarily complicated, the core significance of the progression may become obscured despite the presence of important clinical findings.

Litigation-Ready Output emphasizes clarity without sacrificing physiologic accuracy. The purpose is not to oversimplify medicine.

The purpose is to explain complex clinical progression in a manner that remains understandable, logically connected, and strategically usable under litigation conditions.

This requires more than translating medical terminology into simpler language. The analysis must explain why the progression mattered.

A chronology should not merely state that blood pressure declined. The analysis must explain why the hypotension became clinically significant, how it related to worsening instability, whether escalation opportunity narrowed, and how the deterioration influenced the broader physiologic trajectory.

Similarly, the analysis should not simply identify delayed intervention.

It must explain how the delay interacted with reversibility, progression timing, baseline reserve, operational conditions, and treatment responsiveness throughout the actual sequence of care.

Clarity also strengthens analytical stability.

An analysis that remains logically organized and physiologically understandable is often substantially more resistant to adversarial fragmentation during deposition and cross-examination.

When reasoning pathways become unnecessarily convoluted, internally inconsistent, or excessively dependent upon technical complexity, opposing analysis may more easily isolate weaknesses, create confusion, or challenge the stability of the conclusions themselves.

Litigation-Ready Output requires disciplined communication structure throughout the analysis.

Each conclusion must remain connected to the chronology, the physiology, and the analytic support underlying the opinion itself.

The reader should understand not only what happened, but why it mattered clinically, how the progression evolved, and why the conclusions remain medically sustainable under scrutiny.

Because in medical litigation, clarity is not merely stylistic. Clarity is part of the analytical strength itself.

The Importance Of Internal Consistency

One of the most critical components of Litigation-Ready Output is internal consistency throughout the analysis.

Medical litigation frequently involves thousands of pages of records, multiple providers, evolving physiologic deterioration, competing interpretations, operational complexity, and prolonged chronology progression occurring across different phases of care.

Within that complexity, even strong analyses may weaken substantially if the reasoning becomes internally inconsistent.

A chronology may identify delayed escalation in one section while minimizing the physiologic significance of the deterioration elsewhere. An analysis may criticize reassessment timing while simultaneously acknowledging that instability remained clinically ambiguous during portions of the progression.

Causation conclusions may become overstated relative to the available physiology or inconsistent with the baseline reserve previously established within the case.

When these inconsistencies emerge, the analytical structure itself becomes vulnerable.

Adversarial litigation often focuses less on isolated conclusions and more on whether the reasoning pathway remains stable under scrutiny.

Defense experts may identify inconsistencies between chronology interpretation and causation conclusions. Opposing counsel may isolate portions of the analysis that appear contradictory or physiologically unsupported. Deposition questioning may focus specifically on areas where the reasoning framework shifts, overextends, or departs from the evidence-based record itself.

Litigation-Ready Output requires that every analytical layer remain aligned with the broader progression of care.

Chronology findings must remain consistent with the physiologic analysis. Standard-of-care conclusions must remain connected to what was clinically actionable during the sequence itself. Regulatory findings must align with the operational realities documented within the progression. Causation conclusions must remain proportionate to the available physiology, treatment responsiveness, reversibility, and baseline reserve established throughout the case.

Internal consistency does not require absolute simplicity.

Complex cases may contain competing physiologic explanations, uncertain intervention windows, evolving diagnostic ambiguity, or partially conflicting documentation. However, the analysis must still explain those complexities in a manner that remains logically stable from beginning to end.

This becomes especially important during deposition and expert challenge.

An analysis that changes its physiologic interpretation depending upon which section is being questioned may quickly lose credibility under adversarial review. Similarly, conclusions that extend beyond the available chronology or overstate the significance of the evidence may become increasingly difficult to defend once scrutinized directly.

Litigation-Ready Output emphasizes analytical stability as a foundational component of structured litigation intelligence.

Because in medical litigation, the strength of an opinion depends not only upon whether the conclusions appear persuasive initially, but whether the reasoning supporting those conclusions remains coherent, proportionate, and physiologically consistent under sustained scrutiny.

The Role Of Evidentiary Support

One of the most important requirements within Litigation-Ready Output is evidentiary support.

Medical litigation analysis cannot rely upon assumption, speculation, retrospective frustration, or generalized criticism alone.

Every major conclusion must remain anchored to identifiable chronology findings, documented physiology, operational evidence, treatment progression, or clearly supportable clinical inference grounded within the record itself.

This distinction becomes critically important because litigation analysis eventually operates within an adversarial environment where unsupported conclusions may be challenged directly.

An attorney may initially accept broad clinical concerns at intake. However, during expert review, deposition, mediation, or trial preparation, the analysis must ultimately demonstrate exactly where the evidence supporting each conclusion exists within the progression itself.

A causation opinion unsupported by documented physiology may weaken rapidly under scrutiny. A criticism regarding escalation delay may become vulnerable if the chronology does not clearly establish when the deterioration became clinically actionable. A regulatory concern may lose significance if the operational failure cannot be connected meaningfully to the progression of care.

Litigation-Ready Output requires disciplined evidentiary linkage throughout the analytical structure.

The chronology must support the progression being described.

The physiology must support the causation conclusions being advanced. The operational findings must support the regulatory concerns being identified.

The treatment sequence must support the intervention analysis being presented.

Each analytical conclusion must remain traceable back to identifiable evidence within the record itself.

Evidentiary support does not require absolute certainty.

Medicine frequently involves incomplete documentation, evolving conditions, fragmented reassessment, competing physiologic explanations, and operational ambiguity during active deterioration.

However, the analysis must still remain proportionate to the evidence available.

Conclusions should not extend beyond what the chronology, physiology, and documented progression can reasonably sustain under scrutiny.

This becomes especially important during deposition and cross-examination.

Opposing counsel may isolate unsupported language, identify overstated conclusions, challenge chronology interpretation, or focus attention on areas where the reasoning extends beyond the analytical foundation supporting the opinion itself.

Even clinically persuasive analyses may weaken substantially if the documented structure beneath the conclusions becomes unstable.

Litigation-Ready Output emphasizes fact-based discipline as a foundational component of structured litigation intelligence.

Because in medical litigation, conclusions carry strength only when the underlying evidence remains sufficiently stable to support them under adversarial review.

The Difference Between Advocacy And Analysis

One of the most important distinctions within Litigation-Ready Output is understanding the difference between advocacy and analysis.

Medical litigation naturally involves emotionally charged circumstances.

Patients may suffer catastrophic injury. Families may experience profound loss.

Attorneys may enter cases already convinced that serious wrongdoing occurred.

Clinical records may contain visible delays, fragmented communication, operational failures, or concerning treatment decisions that appear deeply troubling at first review.

However, disciplined litigation analysis cannot rely upon emotional amplification or predetermined conclusions.

The purpose of Litigation-Ready Output is not to force the evidence toward advocacy, it is to evaluate the progression objectively, construct the reasoning carefully, and determine what conclusions the available record can reasonably support under rigorous review.

This distinction becomes critically important because adversarial litigation quickly exposes analyses that appear emotionally driven, overstated, speculative, or disconnected from the actual medical progression.

An opinion may initially appear persuasive when focused primarily upon catastrophic outcome alone. Yet once chronology sequencing, physiologic reserve, treatment responsiveness, operational conditions, and competing disease processes undergo deeper review, portions of the analysis may weaken substantially if the reasoning exceeds what the evidence can sustainably support.

Litigation-Ready Output requires analytical discipline even in highly concerning cases. A devastating outcome does not automatically establish negligence.

A visible deviation does not automatically establish causation.

A delayed intervention does not automatically establish preventability.

The analysis must remain proportionate to the available evidence throughout the progression itself.

Disciplined analysis often strengthens litigation credibility rather than weakening it.

An analysis that acknowledges uncertainty where uncertainty legitimately exists may appear substantially more reliable under adversarial review than one attempting to force certainty beyond what the physiology can reasonably support.

Similarly, recognizing limitations within the chronology, documentation, or causation framework may strengthen the credibility of the conclusions that remain strongly supportable within the case.

This becomes especially important during deposition and expert challenge.

Opposing experts frequently focus upon areas where opinions appear overstated, emotionally reactive, selectively interpreted, or insufficiently supported by the underlying chronology and physiology.

When the reasoning remains measured, internally consistent, evidentiary anchored, and physiologically disciplined, the analysis becomes substantially more resistant to adversarial attack.

Litigation-Ready Output emphasizes objective analytical construction rather than outcome-driven advocacy.

Because in medical litigation, the strongest analyses are often not the most aggressive. They are the most stable under scrutiny.

The Role Of Defensibility Under Scrutiny

One of the central objectives of Litigation-Ready Output is ensuring that the analysis remains defensible under sustained scrutiny.

Medical litigation does not end once conclusions are written.

Every major opinion may eventually undergo deposition examination, competing expert review, evidentiary challenge, defense reinterpretation, judicial evaluation, or adversarial cross-analysis focused specifically on the stability of the reasoning itself.

Analytical stability must be built into the reasoning structure from the beginning.

A chronology may initially appear persuasive during intake review. However, once the analysis enters adversarial litigation, every assumption, causation opinion, operational conclusion, and physiologic interpretation may become subject to direct challenge.

Defense experts may dispute reversibility.

Opposing counsel may challenge chronology sequencing.

Competing interpretations may question whether deterioration was truly actionable at the time intervention allegedly should have occurred. Operational findings may be reframed as reasonable clinical judgment occurring under difficult conditions rather than negligence.

This distinction becomes critically important because litigation analysis must remain stable even when individual portions of the case are isolated and challenged independently.
A strong analysis cannot depend upon broad narrative impression alone.

Each conclusion must remain capable of standing on its own evidentiary and physiologic foundation.

Litigation-Ready Output evaluates not only whether conclusions appear persuasive initially, but whether the reasoning remains proportionate, internally consistent, and medically sustainable once subjected to adversarial pressure.

Analytical durability often depends upon restraint.

Overstated opinions may appear strong initially while becoming increasingly vulnerable during expert review. Conclusions extending beyond the available chronology or physiology may weaken rapidly once opposing analysis focuses attention on evidentiary gaps, competing interpretations, or alternative physiologic explanations.

Conversely, carefully constructed analyses frequently remain more durable under scrutiny because the reasoning remains tightly connected to documented chronology, clinical progression, treatment response, operational evidence, and physiologic plausibility throughout the sequence itself.

This becomes especially important during deposition.

An analysis may contain accurate conclusions yet still become vulnerable if the reasoning pathway appears inconsistent, exaggerated, speculative, or insufficiently supported when questioned in detail over extended examination.

Litigation-Ready Output emphasizes durability of reasoning as much as strength of conclusion.

The analysis must remain capable of withstanding sustained scrutiny without requiring exaggeration, selective interpretation, or unsupported extension beyond what the evidence can reasonably sustain.

Because in medical litigation, defensibility is not established by how aggressively an opinion is written.

It is established by how well the reasoning survives challenge.

The Role Of Deposition Resistance

One of the most important objectives within Litigation-Ready Output is constructing analysis that remains stable during deposition examination.

Medical litigation analysis may initially appear persuasive when reviewed in written form. However, deposition fundamentally changes the environment in which the reasoning is tested.

During deposition, the analysis no longer exists as uninterrupted narrative.

The reasoning becomes fragmented into individual conclusions, isolated chronology points, physiologic interpretations, treatment assumptions, and causation opinions examined one piece at a time under adversarial pressure.

This distinction becomes critically important because even strong clinical analyses may weaken rapidly if the underlying reasoning cannot withstand sustained questioning.

An expert may confidently state that escalation was delayed. Yet deposition may focus specifically on when the deterioration first became clinically actionable, whether competing diagnoses existed, whether instability was clearly recognizable at the time, or whether alternative physiologic explanations reasonably remained possible during the sequence itself.

Similarly, a causation opinion may initially appear compelling until questioning isolates baseline reserve, treatment responsiveness, competing disease processes, delayed presentation, or uncertainty regarding reversibility during the progression itself.

Litigation-Ready Output requires constructing opinions that remain stable even when separated from the broader narrative framework.

Every major conclusion must remain supported independently by chronology, physiology, documented progression, operational evidence, or medically supportable inference grounded within the record itself.

Deposition resistance often depends upon precision of language.

Overly absolute wording may become vulnerable quickly once exceptions, uncertainty, or competing interpretations are introduced during examination. Broad statements unsupported by specific chronology findings may weaken under detailed questioning. Conclusions extending beyond what the physiology reasonably supports may become increasingly difficult to defend once opposing counsel narrows the discussion to isolated portions of the progression.

Conversely, disciplined analytical construction frequently strengthens deposition durability.

An analysis acknowledging uncertainty where uncertainty legitimately exists may remain substantially more credible under sustained questioning than one attempting to force absolute certainty beyond what the evidence can reasonably support.

Similarly, opinions carefully tied to documented chronology, treatment timing, physiologic progression, and documentiary support often remain more resistant to adversarial fragmentation.

This becomes especially important because deposition frequently tests not only the conclusions themselves, but the methodology underlying the analysis.

Opposing counsel may challenge how chronology sequencing was performed, how causation was evaluated, how reversibility was determined, or how operational findings were linked to the progression of care.

Litigation-Ready Output emphasizes methodological stability as much as clinical interpretation.

Because in medical litigation, the strength of an opinion ultimately depends not only upon whether the conclusion appears persuasive initially, but whether the reasoning continues to remain coherent, disciplined, and physiologically sustainable when challenged directly under oath.

The Role Of Strategic Usability

One of the final objectives of Litigation-Ready Output is strategic usability.

Medical analysis may be clinically accurate, physiologically sophisticated, and strategically usable, yet still lose substantial litigation value if the findings cannot be used effectively within legal strategy.

This distinction becomes critically important because litigation analysis does not exist in isolation.

Attorneys must ultimately use the analysis to evaluate liability exposure, assess case strength, prepare expert review, structure deposition questioning, negotiate settlement posture, challenge opposing opinions, prepare mediation strategy, and explain complex medical progression within adversarial proceedings.

Litigation-Ready Output requires more than medical interpretation alone. The analysis must remain operationally usable within the realities of litigation practice. A chronology should not merely describe deterioration.

It should identify where intervention opportunity narrowed, where escalation became clinically actionable, where operational systems weakened, where causation strengthened or weakened, and which portions of the progression carry the greatest strategic significance under scrutiny.

Similarly, causation analysis should not merely conclude that delays existed.

It should explain how timing, reversibility, baseline reserve, treatment responsiveness, and competing physiologic processes influence the strength or vulnerability of the litigation position itself.

This becomes especially important because attorneys often must make major strategic decisions long before formal expert testimony occurs.

Case valuation, settlement consideration, discovery strategy, expert retention, deposition preparation, and litigation risk assessment may all depend heavily upon whether the underlying medical analysis remains organized, understandable, and strategically actionable.

Strategic usability does not mean advocacy-driven presentation. The purpose is not to exaggerate strengths or conceal weaknesses.

In many matters, identifying causation vulnerabilities, evidentiary limitations, chronology inconsistencies, or physiologic uncertainty may become just as strategically important as identifying supportive findings.

A disciplined analysis should clarify where the case is strong, where it remains vulnerable, what conclusions appear sustainable, and which arguments may become difficult to defend under adversarial review.

This is important during mediation and settlement evaluation.

An attorney who clearly understands the physiologic strengths and weaknesses of the case may approach negotiation far differently than one relying primarily upon catastrophic outcome or generalized clinical concern alone.

Litigation-Ready Output emphasizes strategic clarity alongside clinical accuracy.

The analysis must help transform complex medicine into usable litigation intelligence capable of supporting informed legal decision-making throughout the life of the case.

Because in medical litigation, the value of an analysis depends not only upon whether it is medically correct, but whether it can be applied effectively within real-world legal strategy.

CASE ANALYSIS - 1

Strong Clinical Findings With Weak Litigation Structure

A 49-year-old female underwent elective abdominal surgery and initially appeared stable during the early postoperative period. Over the following several hours, the patient developed worsening tachycardia, declining blood pressure, escalating abdominal pain, increasing oxygen requirements, and progressive confusion.

The records contained repeated nursing documentation describing concern regarding worsening instability. Physician communication appeared fragmented throughout portions of the progression, reassessment intervals became inconsistent, and operative reevaluation did not occur until substantially later in the sequence.

At intake, the case appeared highly concerning.

The attorney believed delayed recognition of postoperative hemorrhage contributed directly to the patient's eventual cardiac arrest and catastrophic deterioration.

However, despite the presence of potentially significant findings, the litigation analysis initially remained difficult to defend coherently.

The chronology itself lacked structure.

Critical laboratory trends were separated across multiple documentation systems.

Nursing concerns appeared throughout fragmented charting without clear integration into the physiologic progression. Physician response timing remained difficult to reconstruct precisely. Escalation concerns existed, yet the reasoning pathway connecting deterioration, reassessment failure, delayed intervention, and outcome progression remained operationally unclear.

As a result, the case initially contained important findings without possessing stable litigation organization.

This distinction became highly significant as the analysis deepened.

Because the problem was not necessarily the absence of supportive evidence.

The problem was the absence of a stable analytical framework capable of explaining how the progression unfolded and why the identified failures materially influenced the trajectory of care.

Once the chronology was reconstructed systematically, the progression became substantially clearer.

Vital sign deterioration demonstrated progressive instability over several hours before operative reevaluation occurred. Hemoglobin trends reflected worsening hemorrhagic progression during the delay period. Reassessment intervals narrowed inconsistently despite worsening instability, and portions of the escalation sequence suggested that intervention opportunity may have remained physiologically actionable before irreversible collapse ultimately developed.

The litigation framework strengthened significantly once the physiology, chronology, escalation sequence, and intervention timing were organized into a coherent analytical structure.

The strength of the case did not arise solely from the catastrophic outcome itself.

It arose from the ability to demonstrate - clearly and coherently - how the deterioration evolved, where escalation opportunity narrowed, how the delays influenced the progression, and why the conclusions remained physiologically sustainable under scrutiny.

This distinction became central to the litigation posture.

Because before the analysis was organized, the case contained concerning findings but limited strategic clarity.

Once the chronology, physiology, operational concerns, and causation framework were integrated systematically, the analysis became substantially more usable within litigation strategy.

This is one of the central principles of Litigation-Ready Output within the Lexcura Clinical Intelligence Model™: Strong clinical findings alone do not create strong litigation analysis.

The findings must be organized into a coherent, analytically sound reasoning structure capable of surviving adversarial scrutiny.

CASE ANALYSIS - 2

Clinically Concerning Care With Weak Analytical Stability

A 76-year-old male with advanced congestive heart failure, severe chronic kidney disease, insulin-dependent diabetes, chronic respiratory disease, and recurrent hospitalization history presented with worsening shortness of breath, hypotension, progressive confusion, and signs concerning for evolving septic deterioration.

During the progression, several aspects of care appeared operationally concerning.

Physician reassessment intervals became prolonged during portions of the sequence.

ICU transfer occurred later than expected, documentation continuity weakened as instability progressed, and escalation timing appeared inconsistent throughout the deterioration itself.

At intake, the case initially appeared highly supportive of negligence.

The family strongly believed earlier intervention would have prevented the patient's death, and portions of the chronology appeared visibly concerning during early review.

However, deeper Litigation-Ready Output analysis revealed substantial structural weaknesses within the case itself.

The chronology contained significant ambiguity regarding when the deterioration first became clearly actionable. Multiple competing physiologic processes existed simultaneously throughout the progression, including severe baseline cardiac dysfunction, chronic respiratory compromise, advanced renal impairment, and evidence of progressive multi-organ instability already developing before portions of the delay period occurred.

The causation framework became increasingly difficult to defend consistently under scrutiny.

Although portions of the escalation sequence appeared imperfect, the records also demonstrated that the patient's physiology remained profoundly compromised throughout the progression itself. Treatment responsiveness remained limited despite ICU escalation, vasopressor support, ventilatory management, and aggressive intervention following transfer.

As the analysis deepened, the litigation vulnerabilities became increasingly apparent.

Certain chronology conclusions depended heavily upon retrospective interpretation rather than clearly documented intervention opportunity. Portions of the reassessment criticism became difficult to sustain consistently once the progression was evaluated within the context of the patient's severe baseline instability. Several causation opinions also risked extending beyond what the available physiology could reliably support under adversarial review.

This did not eliminate the presence of clinically concerning care.

The chronology still supported criticism regarding portions of escalation timing, reassessment continuity, and operational response during the deterioration itself.

However, Litigation-Ready Output requires more than identifying concerning care alone. The analysis must remain analytically stable.

As the case underwent deeper reconstruction, the litigation posture weakened because the reasoning pathway supporting causation became increasingly vulnerable to challenge regarding reversibility, baseline reserve, competing physiologic processes, and uncertainty surrounding whether earlier intervention probably would have altered the final outcome.

This distinction became critically important strategically.

Because although the records contained visible operational concerns, the analytical structure supporting sustainable causation remained significantly less stable once subjected to deeper physiologic and evidentiary review.

This is one of the central principles of Litigation-Ready Output within the Lexcura Clinical Intelligence Model™: Clinically concerning care does not automatically create strong litigation positioning.

The analysis must remain coherent, proportionate, and physiologically sustainable.

Applying Litigation-Ready Output

Understanding Litigation-Ready Output conceptually is only the beginning.

The true importance of this pillar becomes apparent when complex medical findings must be transformed into analysis capable of surviving real-world litigation scrutiny.

In practice, Litigation-Ready Output determines whether chronology reconstruction, physiologic analysis, operational findings, standard-of-care evaluation, regulatory concerns, and causation conclusions can be organized into a structure that remains strategically usable and analytically sound under adversarial review.

The analysis therefore evaluates far more than whether concerning care occurred.

It examines whether the reasoning itself remains coherent, internally consistent, legally supported, physiologically sustainable, and operationally stable once challenged through deposition, competing expert interpretation, or litigation strategy review.

The following exercise is designed to apply these principles within a realistic medical litigation setting.

As you review the chronology, it is important to evaluate not only whether clinically concerning findings exist, but whether the analytical structure supporting those conclusions remains defensible under scrutiny.

Consider whether the chronology is sufficiently organized to support the progression being described. Evaluate whether the causation framework remains proportionate to the available physiology. Consider whether the operational concerns are meaningfully connected to the deterioration itself, whether the conclusions remain evidentiary anchored, and whether the reasoning pathway can withstand adversarial challenge without becoming fragmented or internally inconsistent.

This distinction forms one of the central analytical foundations of the Lexcura Clinical Intelligence Model™.

Because in medical litigation, identifying important findings alone is never sufficient. The analysis must ultimately transform those findings into organized litigation intelligence capable of supporting real-world legal strategy under sustained scrutiny.

Evaluating Defensibility Within a Progressive Deterioration Chronology

A 62-year-old female underwent abdominal surgery and initially appeared stable during the postoperative period. Over the following several hours, the patient developed worsening tachycardia, declining blood pressure, increasing abdominal pain, progressive confusion, worsening oxygen requirements, and laboratory findings concerning for evolving postoperative hemorrhage.

Nursing documentation reflected repeated concern regarding progressive instability throughout portions of the sequence. Reassessment intervals became inconsistent during the deterioration, physician communication appeared fragmented, and operative reevaluation did not occur until substantially later in the progression itself.

The patient eventually experienced cardiac arrest requiring emergent intervention, massive transfusion, and operative exploration confirming significant postoperative hemorrhage.

At intake, the chronology appeared highly supportive of delayed recognition and escalation failure.

However, deeper Litigation-Ready Output analysis revealed several important structural questions requiring evaluation.

The chronology itself remained fragmented across multiple documentation systems. Portions of the escalation timeline were difficult to reconstruct precisely.

Certain reassessment concerns appeared physiologically important, yet some operational criticisms relied heavily upon retrospective interpretation rather than clearly documented intervention opportunity during the actual progression itself.

At the same time, the records also demonstrated progressive vital sign instability, worsening laboratory trends, narrowing intervention opportunity, and escalating physiologic deterioration occurring over several hours before definitive operative intervention ultimately occurred.

As part of the Lexcura Clinical Intelligence Model™, your task is to evaluate whether the available analysis remains sufficiently organized, well-supported, physiologically coherent, and strategically sound to withstand adversarial scrutiny within active medical litigation.

Answer Key & Analysis

The central analytical issue in this case is not simply whether the patient ultimately experienced catastrophic postoperative hemorrhagic deterioration.

The deeper issue is whether the litigation analysis itself remains sufficiently organized, physiologically coherent, fact-based supported, and defensible under adversarial scrutiny.

At first review, the chronology appears highly concerning.

The patient demonstrated progressive hypotension, worsening tachycardia, increasing oxygen requirements, escalating abdominal pain, progressive confusion, and laboratory abnormalities concerning for evolving hemorrhagic instability over several hours before definitive operative intervention ultimately occurred.

Nursing documentation reflected repeated concern regarding worsening deterioration, reassessment intervals became inconsistent during portions of the progression, and physician communication appeared fragmented throughout the sequence itself.

An attorney initially reviewing the records may reasonably conclude that delayed recognition and escalation substantially contributed to the patient's cardiac arrest and catastrophic deterioration.

However, deeper Litigation-Ready Output analysis requires evaluating not only whether concerning findings exist, but whether the reasoning pathway supporting those conclusions remains stable under scrutiny.

The chronology ultimately demonstrated objective physiologic evidence supporting progressive hemorrhagic deterioration during the sequence itself.

Vital sign instability worsened progressively throughout the delay period. Laboratory trends supported evolving blood loss physiology. The patient's deterioration became increasingly actionable over time, and operative exploration eventually confirmed significant postoperative hemorrhage requiring emergent intervention.

This distinction substantially strengthens the analytical framework.

Because the conclusions do not rely solely upon retrospective dissatisfaction with the outcome itself.

The chronology, physiology, and operative findings collectively support a progression in which meaningful intervention opportunity likely remained present during portions of the deterioration.

At the same time, portions of the litigation structure still require analytical restraint.

Certain reassessment criticisms depend partially upon fragmented documentation and retrospective chronology reconstruction rather than uninterrupted contemporaneous escalation evidence throughout every phase of the progression.

Some operational criticisms may also become vulnerable if overstated beyond what the available chronology can consistently support under detailed scrutiny.

The strongest litigation posture remains tightly connected to the most physiologically stable portions of the progression itself.

The analysis becomes strongest when focused upon the objectively worsening instability, narrowing intervention opportunity, delayed operative reevaluation, progressive hemorrhagic physiology, and eventual confirmation of significant postoperative bleeding rather than relying upon speculative assumptions regarding every individual provider decision occurring during the sequence.

The confirmed postoperative hemorrhage materially strengthens causation analysis.

Because the operative findings support that the deterioration reflected an active and evolving physiologic process occurring during the progression itself rather than purely retrospective reinterpretation after the outcome became known.

The chronology therefore supports a credible argument that earlier recognition, escalation, reassessment continuity, and operative intervention may reasonably have altered the physiologic trajectory before irreversible collapse ultimately developed.

The litigation framework remains substantially more stable once the litigation structure is integrated into a coherent analytical structure rather than presented as isolated criticisms.

The strength of the case does not arise solely from the catastrophic outcome.

It arises from the ability to demonstrate - clearly, proportionately, and physiologically how the deterioration evolved, where intervention opportunity narrowed, how the delays influenced the progression, and why the conclusions remain sustainable under adversarial scrutiny.

This is one of the central principles of Litigation-Ready Output within the Lexcura Clinical Intelligence Model™: Strong litigation analysis depends not only upon identifying concerning clinical findings, but upon organizing those findings into a coherent, record-supported, and physiologically defensible reasoning structure capable of surviving challenge.

Chapter 7 Takeaways

Litigation-Ready Output

1. *Strong clinical findings alone do not create strong litigation analysis.*

The findings must be organized into a coherent reasoning structure capable of surviving adversarial scrutiny.

2. *Clinical review and litigation analysis are not the same process.*

Litigation analysis requires chronology reconstruction, physiologic linkage, evidentiary support, and sustainable causation evaluation rather than retrospective clinical concern alone.

3. *Analytical structure directly influences litigation strength.*

Even important findings may weaken substantially if the reasoning pathway becomes fragmented, inconsistent, disorganized, or difficult to follow.

4. *Clarity strengthens both communication and defensibility.*

Complex medical progression must remain understandable, logically connected, and strategically usable without sacrificing physiologic accuracy.

5. *Internal consistency is essential to analytical stability.*

Chronology findings, causation conclusions, operational analysis, and physiologic interpretation must remain aligned throughout the progression itself.

6. *Every major conclusion requires evidentiary support.*

Litigation analysis must remain anchored to identifiable chronology findings, documented physiology, operational evidence, and medically supportable inference.

7. *Advocacy cannot replace disciplined analysis.*

Emotionally driven conclusions, speculative interpretation, and overstated causation frequently weaken defensibility under scrutiny.

8. *Defensibility depends upon analytical restraint*

The strongest analyses often remain tightly connected to what the chronology, physiology, and evidentiary record can reasonably sustain.

9. Deposition resistance requires methodological stability.

Each conclusion must remain capable of surviving adversarial fragmentation, detailed questioning, and competing expert interpretation.

10. Strategic usability is part of litigation value.

Medical analysis must ultimately support real-world legal strategy including case evaluation, expert review, deposition preparation, mediation, and settlement analysis.

11. Litigation-Ready Output transforms analysis into usable litigation intelligence.

Chronology reconstruction, standard-of-care analysis, regulatory evaluation, and causation mapping must function together within one coherent analytical framework

12. The strength of litigation analysis depends upon the stability of the reasoning itself.

Before medical findings can influence legal outcome, the analysis must remain coherent, physiologically sustainable, evidence-based, and defensible under adversarial assessment.

Transition To The Final Phase Of The Model

Once Litigation-Ready Output has transformed complex medical findings into organized and defensible litigation intelligence, the final phase of the Lexcura Clinical Intelligence Model™ becomes fully visible.

At this stage, the objective is no longer simply understanding what happened medically.

The objective becomes understanding how the analysis itself influences liability exposure, litigation positioning, settlement evaluation, expert strategy, deposition preparation, evidentiary strength, and overall case direction under adversarial scrutiny.

This is where the Lexcura Clinical Intelligence Model™ fundamentally separates itself from traditional medical record review.

The model is not designed merely to identify isolated deviations, summarize chronology events, or highlight concerning documentation.

It is designed to construct a clinically disciplined, physiologically coherent, strategically usable litigation framework capable of supporting real-world legal decision-making.

Every prior pillar contributes directly to this final integration.

Record Integrity establishes whether the documentation itself remains reliable enough to support structured analysis. Baseline Profiling defines the patient's physiologic condition before deterioration developed. Timeline Reconstruction organizes how instability evolved throughout the sequence of care. Standard-of-Care Analysis evaluates where clinical expectations emerged and whether departures occurred.

Regulatory & Compliance Overlay examines how operational systems influenced the progression. Causation Mapping determines whether the identified failures probably altered the physiologic trajectory during a period when meaningful reversibility still realistically existed.

Litigation-Ready Output then transforms those findings into organized litigation intelligence capable of surviving adversarial scrutiny.

Together, these pillars create far more than retrospective case review.

They create an integrated clinical intelligence methodology specifically structured for medical litigation analysis.

Medical litigation is inherently adversarial.

Cases strengthen or weaken based upon whether the chronology, physiology, operational conditions, causation framework, evidentiary support, and strategic reasoning remain internally coherent when examined together under scrutiny.

Because the Lexcura Clinical Intelligence Model™ functions as an integrated analytical system rather than a collection of disconnected review concepts. Each pillar reinforces the stability of the others.

Weak chronology weakens causation. Weak causation weakens strategic usability.

Weak evidentiary support weakens defensibility. Strong analytical integration, however, creates litigation intelligence capable of supporting sustainable legal strategy.

This is the central objective of the Lexcura Clinical Intelligence Model™.

Not merely identifying concerning medicine.

But transforming complex clinical progression into structured, disciplined, physiologically grounded litigation intelligence capable of influencing real-world legal outcome.

CHAPTER - 08

CLINICAL INTELLIGENCE

Advancing structured clinical intelligence
or the next generation of medical-legal analysis.

This chapter establishes a foundational pillar within the Lexcura Clinical Intelligence Model™ creating the evidentiary framework required for defensible medical-legal analysis.

THE FUTURE OF CLINICAL INTELLIGENCE IN MEDICAL LITIGATION

Medical litigation has become increasingly complex.

Modern healthcare systems involve fragmented documentation, overlapping specialties, evolving operational structures, rapidly changing physiology, extensive electronic records, layered regulatory expectations, and increasingly sophisticated standards surrounding causation, escalation, communication, and patient safety.

As this complexity has expanded, traditional approaches to medical record review have often struggled to keep pace.

Chronologies may summarize events without explaining physiologic significance.

Standard-of-care review may identify isolated deviations without integrating operational context or causation analysis. Regulatory concerns may be identified without demonstrating how those failures materially influenced the progression.

Catastrophic outcomes may generate emotionally persuasive narratives while lacking sustainable physiologic linkage between the alleged failures and the ultimate injury.

As a result, large volumes of medical information frequently produce unclear litigation analysis rather than coherent litigation intelligence.

This is one of the central problems the Lexcura Clinical Intelligence Model™ was designed to address.

Medical records alone do not create litigation strength. Information alone is not enough.

The central issue is whether the progression can be organized into a coherent analytical structure capable of explaining how the deterioration unfolded and why the conclusions remain sustainable.

This distinction fundamentally changes how medical litigation analysis is approached.

The purpose of the Lexcura Clinical Intelligence Model™ is not simply to identify concerning medicine in hindsight.

It is to reconstruct the progression systematically, evaluate the surrounding operational environment, determine where intervention opportunities emerged or narrowed, analyze whether identified failures materially influenced the physiologic trajectory, and organize those findings into structured litigation intelligence capable of supporting meaningful legal strategy.

The strength of the model comes from integration.

Record Integrity establishes whether the documentation itself remains reliable enough to support meaningful analysis. Baseline Profiling defines the patient's physiologic condition before deterioration developed.

Timeline Reconstruction organizes how instability evolved throughout the sequence of care. Standard-of-Care Analysis evaluates where clinical expectations emerged and whether departures occurred. Regulatory & Compliance Overlay examines how operational systems influenced the progression.

Causation Mapping determines whether the identified failures probably altered the patient's physiologic trajectory during a period when meaningful reversibility still realistically existed. Litigation-Ready Output then transforms those findings into coherent litigation intelligence capable of supporting strategic decision-making.

Individually, each pillar provides analytical value.

Together, they create a structured clinical intelligence methodology designed specifically for the realities of medical litigation.

This distinction becomes increasingly important as healthcare systems continue evolving.

Modern litigation rarely involves simple factual disputes alone. Cases often require evaluation of progressive physiologic deterioration occurring across timelines, multiple providers, operational strain, competing disease processes, delayed recognition, incomplete reassessment, documentation inconsistency, evolving standards, and layered causation questions developing simultaneously throughout the progression.

Isolated review methods frequently become insufficient. Chronology alone is not enough.

Causation alone is not enough. Regulatory review alone is not enough.

The analytical value emerges through disciplined integration of all components of the progression.

This is where clinical intelligence becomes fundamentally different from traditional retrospective review.

The purpose is not merely to criticize outcomes. The purpose is to understand progression.

Why did the deterioration evolve the way it did? When did intervention opportunity realistically exist? What operational conditions influenced the sequence?

Which findings carry true causation significance?

Which conclusions remain proportionate to the available physiology?

Which portions of the case strengthen or weaken once the progression undergoes deeper analysis?

These questions require more than generalized review. They require structured analysis.

Importantly, the Lexcura Clinical Intelligence Model™ is not built upon emotional amplification, hindsight accusation, or predetermined litigation positioning. The model is built upon analytical discipline.

Strong cases remain strong because the chronology, physiology, operational findings, and causation framework remain coherent when examined together.

Weak cases remain weak even when outcomes appear emotionally compelling if the progression cannot sustain the conclusions being advanced.

Medical litigation ultimately depends upon stability of reasoning.

An opinion may initially appear persuasive. However, once chronology sequencing, baseline reserve, treatment responsiveness, operational context, competing physiologic explanations, and evidentiary support undergo deeper examination, the analytical structure must continue holding together.

That is where disciplined methodology becomes essential.

The future of medical litigation analysis will increasingly depend upon integrated clinical intelligence rather than isolated retrospective review.

Healthcare systems are becoming more operationally complex. Electronic medical records continue expanding in volume. Litigation strategy increasingly depends upon integrated clinical analysis rather than isolated criticism alone.

Under those conditions, sustainable litigation analysis requires structure. It requires disciplined reasoning.

It requires physiologic coherence.

And it requires analytical methods capable of transforming large volumes of fragmented medical information into organized litigation intelligence that remains strategically usable within the realities of modern litigation practice.

This is the purpose of the Lexcura Clinical Intelligence Model™.

Not simply reviewing records.

But transforming complex clinical progression into structured, disciplined, physiologically grounded litigation intelligence capable of supporting clear, sustainable, and strategically usable medical analysis.

The Difference Between Information And Intelligence

Once of the central problems in medical litigation is that healthcare records often contain enormous amounts of information while providing very little true understanding of what actually happened during the progression of care.

Modern medical records may span thousands of pages across multiple admissions, specialties, consultant evaluations, nursing notes, operative reports, laboratory trends, medication records, imaging findings, reassessment documentation, and disconnected communication entries occurring over days, weeks, or even months.

Yet despite the sheer volume of documentation, the actual clinical progression may still remain difficult to understand clearly.

Important physiologic changes may be buried across disconnected portions of the record. Escalation timing may remain unclear. Operational failures may appear partially visible without being fully connected to the deterioration itself.

Critical causation questions may exist within the chronology but remain obscured beneath extensive documentation volume and unclear sequencing.

As a result, large medical records frequently create informational overload rather than meaningful litigation clarity.

This is one of the foundational distinctions within the Lexcura Clinical Intelligence Model™.

Medical records contain information. Clinical intelligence creates understanding.

Information alone does not explain why deterioration progressed the way it did, when meaningful intervention opportunity realistically existed, which findings materially influenced the trajectory, how operational conditions affected the sequence, or whether the conclusions remain proportionate to the available physiology.

Those questions require integration.

This is why chronology alone is often insufficient.

A chronology may accurately describe what occurred without explaining why the progression mattered physiologically or strategically within the broader litigation framework.

Similarly, isolated standard-of-care criticism may identify deviations without determining whether those deviations actually altered the patient's trajectory.

Regulatory concerns may identify operational weaknesses without establishing whether those failures materially influenced the deterioration itself. Catastrophic outcomes may create emotionally persuasive narratives while remaining physiologically weak once causation undergoes deeper analysis.

Clinical intelligence therefore requires more than retrospective record review. It requires disciplined reconstruction of the progression.

The analysis must organize the broader clinical progression into a coherent framework capable of explaining how the progression unfolded and why the conclusions remain analytically stable.

This is where the Lexcura Clinical Intelligence Model™ differs fundamentally from isolated retrospective review.

The model does not treat each component of the analysis as an isolated process operating independently from one another.

Each pillar influences the others.

Weak chronology weakens causation. Weak causation weakens litigation positioning.

Weak evidentiary support weakens analytical stability. Strong integration, however, creates organized litigation intelligence capable of supporting meaningful legal strategy.

Importantly, this distinction extends beyond litigation outcomes alone.

Integrated clinical intelligence also strengthens analytical discipline itself. The model requires the progression to remain internally coherent. It forces conclusions to remain proportionate to the available physiology. It reduces reliance upon hindsight amplification and emotionally driven interpretation. It strengthens the ability to identify both supportive findings and structural weaknesses within the same case.

This becomes increasingly important as healthcare systems continue growing more operationally and clinically complex.

Medical litigation no longer depends upon isolated documentation review alone.

It increasingly requires structured analytical methods capable of transforming large volumes of medical information into clear understanding of progression, causation, operational influence, and litigation significance.

That transformation - from information into intelligence - is one of the central purposes of the Lexcura Clinical Intelligence Model™.

Why Clinical Complexity Requires Structure

Modern medical litigation rarely involves simple clinical sequences.

Patients frequently deteriorate through overlapping physiologic processes occurring across complex timelines, multiple providers, shifting operational conditions, incomplete reassessments, evolving treatment decisions, and competing diagnostic possibilities developing simultaneously throughout the progression of care.

Under these conditions, isolated review methods often become insufficient.

A delay may appear significant until baseline physiology is examined more closely. A concerning outcome may initially appear preventable until treatment responsiveness, reversibility, or competing disease processes undergo deeper analysis.

Operational failures may appear highly damaging until chronology reconstruction clarifies whether those failures materially influenced the progression.

This is why medical litigation cannot rely solely upon isolated chronology review, generalized standard-of-care criticism, or retrospective outcome interpretation.

Complex clinical progression requires structure.

Without structure, important findings may remain disconnected from the broader physiologic sequence. Escalation concerns may become separated from intervention opportunity.

Operational failures may be identified without determining whether they materially influenced causation. Chronology detail may overwhelm the analysis without clarifying why the progression unfolded the way it did.

As a result, the litigation framework may lose coherence even when the records contain clinically important findings.

The Lexcura Clinical Intelligence Model™ was designed specifically to address this problem.

The purpose of the model is not simply to collect information.

It is to organize complex clinical progression into an integrated analytical structure capable of explaining how deterioration evolved, which factors materially influenced the sequence, where intervention opportunity emerged or narrowed, and whether the conclusions remain proportionate to the available physiology.

Modern healthcare systems themselves continue becoming increasingly complex.

Patients often receive care across multiple departments, facilities, specialties, and provider teams. Documentation may be distributed across extensive electronic medical record systems containing thousands of fragmented entries.

Operational conditions may fluctuate significantly throughout the progression. Reassessment timing, escalation structure, staffing conditions, communication reliability, and treatment responsiveness may all influence the sequence simultaneously.

Meaningful litigation analysis requires more than identifying isolated concerns within the record.

It requires disciplined integration of the progression.

This is where structured clinical intelligence becomes essential.

The analysis must determine not only what happened, but why it mattered physiologically, operationally, and strategically within the broader progression of care.

That process requires integrated clinical analysis rather than isolated review methods to function together rather than independently.

Without that integration, medical litigation analysis risks becoming reactive rather than analytical.

The conclusions may appear persuasive initially while weakening substantially once chronology sequencing, operational context, competing physiology, or causation significance undergo deeper examination.

Structured methodology helps prevent that loss of coherence.

It forces the analysis to remain internally coherent and tied to the underlying progression rather than retrospective assumption alone.

This is one of the central reasons the Lexcura Clinical Intelligence Model™ functions as an integrated analytical system rather than a collection of isolated review concepts. Because modern medical litigation complexity requires more than information.

It requires structure capable of transforming complex clinical progression into coherent litigation intelligence.

Answer Key & Analysis

One of the most important principles within the Lexcura Clinical Intelligence Model™ is that strong medical litigation analysis depends upon clinical discipline rather than retrospective amplification.

Medical records frequently contain emotionally compelling outcomes. Patients may suffer catastrophic deterioration, permanent injury, profound neurologic loss, or death following sequences that appear highly concerning during initial review.

Families may understandably believe the progression should have been prevented. Attorneys may enter the case already convinced that serious failures occurred.

However, disciplined clinical intelligence requires more than identifying emotionally persuasive facts.

It requires determining what the progression can actually support once the broader progression undergoes deeper analysis.

Emotionally compelling outcomes do not automatically establish strong litigation positioning.

A delay may appear highly concerning while carrying limited causation significance once baseline reserve and reversibility are examined more closely. A deviation may appear substantial until chronology reconstruction clarifies that irreversible deterioration had already progressed before meaningful intervention opportunity realistically existed.

Operational concerns may initially seem highly damaging until the broader physiologic sequence demonstrates that the outcome probably would not have changed despite earlier intervention.

Conversely, relatively subtle failures may become highly significant when they materially alter the progression during a period in which meaningful reversibility still existed.

This is why disciplined analysis matters.

The Lexcura Clinical Intelligence Model™ is not designed to force conclusions toward predetermined litigation outcomes.

The model is designed to evaluate the progression proportionately.

Strong cases remain strong because the progression remains coherent under deeper analysis when examined together. Weak cases remain weak even when the outcomes appear emotionally compelling if the progression cannot sustain the conclusions being advanced.

This principle requires restraint.

Not every documentation inconsistency carries major litigation significance. Not every delayed reassessment materially alters causation. Not every operational weakness meaningfully influences patient outcome. And not every catastrophic deterioration was realistically preventable within the conditions that existed during the actual progression of care.

Disciplined clinical intelligence therefore requires the ability to identify both strengths and limitations within the same case.

The analysis must remain proportionate to the underlying progression and available physiology rather than retrospective assumption. Causation opinions must remain connected to realistic intervention opportunity, treatment responsiveness, reversibility, and baseline reserve rather than outcome severity alone.

This becomes increasingly important in modern medical litigation because retrospective interpretation naturally creates pressure toward oversimplification.

Once the final outcome becomes known, earlier findings may appear more obvious, actionable, or preventable than they realistically appeared during the actual progression. Chronology reconstruction may unintentionally become influenced by hindsight rather than real-time clinical conditions.

Operational concerns may appear more significant retrospectively than they functioned within the evolving sequence of care.

Clinical discipline helps prevent that distortion.
It forces the analysis to remain grounded in the progression rather than retrospective emotional interpretation.

This is one of the central strengths of the Lexcura Clinical Intelligence Model™.
The model does not rely upon amplification.

It relies upon structure, integration, physiologic coherence, and disciplined reasoning capable of sustaining meaningful litigation analysis within increasingly complex healthcare environments.

Final Integration Of The Model

The Lexcura Clinical Intelligence Model™ was developed from one central recognition: Medical litigation requires more than retrospective record review.

Modern healthcare progression is too clinically and operationally complex to be understood through isolated chronology critique, generalized standard-of-care analysis, or outcome-driven interpretation alone.

Meaningful litigation analysis requires integration.

When chronology, causation, operational context, and evidentiary analysis are reviewed independently, the broader framework often loses coherence. Concerning findings may be identified without clarifying physiologic significance, causation linkage, or strategic relevance within the progression.

This lack of integration remains one of the central weaknesses of traditional retrospective review.

The Lexcura Clinical Intelligence Model™ was designed to address that problem through structured clinical intelligence.

Each pillar serves a distinct analytical purpose while strengthening the broader framework as a whole. Together, the model integrates documentation integrity, baseline physiology, chronology reconstruction, standard-of-care evaluation, operational analysis, causation assessment, and litigation strategy into one disciplined methodology designed for modern medical litigation complexity.

Importantly, the model is not designed to amplify criticism or predetermine litigation outcome. Its purpose is disciplined understanding.

Why did the deterioration progress the way it did? Where did meaningful intervention opportunity realistically exist? Which findings materially influenced the sequence?

Which conclusions remain proportionate once the progression undergoes deeper physiologic and evidentiary analysis?

These questions require more than isolated review concepts. They require integrated clinical intelligence.

Healthcare systems continue evolving in both clinical and operational complexity.

Medical records continue expanding in size and complexity. Operational systems remain increasingly layered, and litigation strategy increasingly depends upon disciplined analytical integration rather than isolated criticism alone.

Meaningful medical litigation analysis requires structure capable of transforming complex clinical information into analytical clarity of progression, causation, operational influence, and strategic significance.

That is the central purpose of the Lexcura Clinical Intelligence Model™.

To transform complex clinical progression into structured, disciplined, physiologically coherent litigation intelligence capable of supporting sustainable medical-legal analysis within the realities of modern litigation practice.

Closing Reflection

Medical litigation ultimately depends upon understanding progression. Not isolated documentation entries.

Not retrospective outcome interpretation.

Not isolated criticism viewed independently from the broader clinical sequence.

The central challenge is determining how the broader clinical progression unfolded throughout the actual progression of care.

That process requires more than information alone.

It requires disciplined clinical intelligence.

The Lexcura Clinical Intelligence Model™ was developed to provide that structure.

The model recognizes that meaningful medical litigation analysis must remain physiologically coherent, operationally informed, analytically disciplined, and strategically usable within the realities of modern healthcare and litigation complexity.

Modern medical records often contain enormous amounts of information while providing very little organized understanding of what the progression actually means.

Important findings may remain buried within disconnected documentation.

Causation may appear persuasive initially while weakening under deeper physiologic analysis.

Operational failures may seem highly significant until chronology reconstruction clarifies their actual influence on the sequence itself. Catastrophic outcomes may create emotionally compelling narratives while remaining analytically unstable once the broader progression undergoes disciplined review.

The Lexcura Clinical Intelligence Model™ was designed to reduce that analytical disconnect.

Not by simplifying complexity.

But by organizing complexity into a coherent analytical structure capable of explaining how the progression unfolded and why the conclusions remain proportionate to the available evidence and physiology.

This requires discipline.

The model does not rely upon amplification, hindsight accusation, or predetermined litigation positioning.

It relies upon structured clinical integration, evidentiary support, and analytical coherence functioning together within one integrated framework.

Strong cases remain strong because the progression sustains the conclusions being advanced.

Weak cases remain weak even when the outcomes are emotionally compelling if the chronology, physiology, operational context, or causation framework cannot support the reasoning consistently.

This is one of the most important distinctions within modern medical litigation analysis. The objective is not simply identifying concerning medicine.

The objective is determining whether the progression supports meaningful, sustainable, and strategically usable conclusions once the entire clinical sequence undergoes disciplined evaluation.

As healthcare systems continue becoming more operationally and clinically complex, the need for integrated clinical intelligence will continue expanding.

Medical litigation increasingly requires structured methodology capable of transforming complex medical information into clear understanding of progression, causation, operational influence, and litigation significance.

That is the central purpose of the Lexcura Clinical Intelligence Model™.

To transform complex clinical progression into organized, disciplined, physiologically grounded litigation intelligence capable of supporting meaningful medical-legal analysis within the realities of modern litigation practice.

Final Principles Of The Lexcura Clinical Intelligence Model™

The Lexcura Clinical Intelligence Model™ is ultimately built upon one foundational principle: Medical litigation analysis must remain anchored to the actual clinical progression.

The strength of a case does not arise solely from catastrophic outcome, emotionally compelling facts, isolated deviations, or retrospective criticism viewed independently from the broader sequence of care.

Meaningful litigation analysis depends upon whether the broader analytical framework remains coherent when evaluated together as an integrated progression. This requires discipline.

The model does not assume that every poor outcome establishes negligence. It does not assume that every operational failure materially altered causation. It does not assume that hindsight interpretation accurately reflects the real-time clinical conditions providers faced during the progression.

Instead, the model requires the analysis to remain proportionate to the available physiology, chronology, operational evidence, and intervention opportunity present during the actual sequence of care.

Healthcare systems continue growing more complex.

Modern litigation frequently involves overlapping disease processes, fragmented electronic records, multiple providers, operational strain, evolving reassessment findings, competing physiologic explanations, delayed intervention questions, and layered causation issues developing simultaneously throughout the progression.

Meaningful analysis requires more than generalized review.

It requires structured clinical intelligence capable of organizing complexity into analytical clarity.

The Lexcura Clinical Intelligence Model™ was designed to provide that structure.

The model integrates the major components of medical litigation analysis into one disciplined analytical methodology capable of evaluating how deterioration evolved and whether the conclusions remain sustainable once the progression undergoes deeper review.

Importantly, the model also recognizes that strong analysis requires restraint.

Not every deviation carries major litigation significance. Not every delay materially influences outcome. Not every operational weakness alters the patient's trajectory.

And not every catastrophic deterioration was realistically preventable within the physiologic and operational conditions that existed during the progression.

Disciplined clinical intelligence therefore requires the ability to identify both strengths and limitations within the same case.

The analysis must remain internally coherent. Conclusions must remain tied to identifiable chronology findings, physiologic progression, operational evidence, and realistic intervention opportunity.

Causation must remain grounded in reversibility, treatment responsiveness, baseline reserve, and sustainable physiologic reasoning rather than retrospective outcome interpretation alone.

This is what separates integrated clinical intelligence from isolated retrospective review. The purpose is not merely to review records.

The purpose is to understand progression.

Why did the deterioration evolve the way it did? Which findings materially influenced the sequence?

Where did meaningful intervention opportunity realistically exist?

Which conclusions remain proportionate once the progression undergoes disciplined analysis?

These questions define meaningful medical litigation analysis within increasingly complex healthcare environments. That is the central purpose of the Lexcura Clinical Intelligence Model™.

To transform fragmented medical information into organized, disciplined, physiologically coherent litigation intelligence capable of supporting meaningful, sustainable, and strategically usable medical-legal analysis.

Conclusion

Modern medical litigation increasingly demands more than retrospective review alone.

Healthcare progression is now shaped by layered operational systems, fragmented electronic records, evolving standards of care, overlapping disease processes, complex causation questions, and rapidly changing physiologic conditions developing simultaneously throughout the sequence of care.

Isolated review methods often become insufficient.

Chronology alone cannot fully explain progression.

Standard-of-care analysis alone cannot fully explain causation. Regulatory review alone cannot fully explain operational influence.

And catastrophic outcome alone cannot determine whether meaningful intervention opportunity realistically existed during the progression.

Meaningful litigation analysis requires integration.

This is the central principle underlying the Lexcura Clinical Intelligence Model™.

The model was designed to organize complex medical information into coherent clinical understanding capable of explaining how deterioration evolved, which findings materially influenced the sequence, where intervention opportunity emerged or narrowed, and whether the conclusions remain proportionate to the available physiology and evidence.

This process requires discipline.

The analysis must remain grounded in the underlying progression and available physiology, reversibility, baseline reserve, and sustainable causation reasoning rather than hindsight amplification or emotionally driven interpretation alone.

Strong cases remain strong because the progression continues supporting the conclusions being advanced once the records undergo deeper evaluation.

Weak cases remain weak even when outcomes are catastrophic if the broader progression cannot sustain the reasoning consistently. This distinction is one of the defining principles of modern clinical intelligence.

The purpose is not merely identifying concerning medicine in hindsight.

The purpose is understanding progression with enough structure, discipline, and physiologic coherence to transform complex medical information into strategically usable litigation intelligence.

As healthcare systems continue becoming more clinically and operationally complex, the need for integrated clinical intelligence will continue expanding.

Medical litigation increasingly requires analytical methodology capable of organizing complex clinical progression into clear understanding of causation, operational influence, intervention opportunity, and litigation significance.

The purpose of the Lexcura Clinical Intelligence Model™ is not merely to review records, but to transform complex clinical progression into organized, disciplined, physiologically grounded litigation intelligence capable of supporting meaningful medical-legal analysis within the realities of modern litigation practice.

www.ingramcontent.com/pod-product-compliance
Lightning Source LLC
LaVergne TN
LVHW051133210926
848482LV00006B/301